Stop Washing the Sheets

How to Cure Your Child's Bedwetting

Dr. Lane Robson

iUniverse, Inc.
Bloomington

Stop Washing the Sheets
How to Cure Your Child's Bedwetting

iUniverse books may be ordered through booksellers or by contacting:

iUniverse
1663 Liberty Drive
Bloomington, IN 47403
www.iuniverse.com
1-800-Authors (1-800-288-4677)

Because of the dynamic nature of the Internet, any web addresses or links contained in this book may have changed since publication and may no longer be valid. The views expressed in this work are solely those of the author and do not necessarily reflect the views of the publisher, and the publisher hereby disclaims any responsibility for them.

Any people depicted in stock imagery provided by Thinkstock are models, and such images are being used for illustrative purposes only.

Certain stock imagery © Thinkstock.

ISBN: 978-1-4620-0265-8 (sc)
ISBN: 978-1-4620-0267-2 (hc)
ISBN: 978-1-4620-0266-5 (e)

Printed in the United States of America

iUniverse rev. date: 9/21/2011

Contents

Preface

The first time I tried to write this book was fourteen years ago in 1996. At that time, I was forty-six years old and the head of paediatric nephrology (specialist in kidney problems in children) for a children's hospital in the United States.

Every paediatric kidney specialist treats children with bedwetting. Some enjoy helping children and families with this problem, and others clearly don't. Bedwetting is not a glamorous problem to assess for many of my colleagues.

When I finished my fellowship in paediatric nephrology at the University of Toronto in 1979, I returned to Calgary and founded the division of paediatric nephrology at the University of Calgary. Children with bedwetting were referred to me, and I recollect feeling very helpless when I saw these children. I had no idea how to help. At that time, very little was known about the causes of bedwetting, and my years at Sick Kids in Toronto had offered very little information on the subject. I was very skilled at uncommon problems, such as kidney failure, dialysis, and transplantation, but I didn't know much about bedwetting.

I recollect the first time I prescribed a bedwetting alarm. The memory is vivid. I had no experience with alarms, but I had read that alarms might help. I told a mother to buy an alarm. She returned a month later mad at me.

"I paid seventy-five dollars for that stupid alarm, and he never woke up. I wasted that money."

I can still see her sitting in my office. Her look humbled me.

I agreed with her then, and I agree with her now. I had no business prescribing something that I knew nothing about—or, for that matter, treating a problem that I really knew so little about.

My personality is such that a helpless feeling needs to be resolved, and I decided to learn as much as I could about bedwetting. I read all the available medical papers on the subject. Fairly soon after that, I had two four-inch-thick blue binders filled with papers. Today, I have about forty similar binders devoted to the subject.

Twenty-three years ago, in 1987, I published my first paper on bedwetting—"Nocturnal Enuresis: A Common Frustration." I recollect thinking at the time that I was not sure who was more frustrated: the children and parents for having the problem or me for my inability to solve it.

There were lots of kidney and bladder problems in children that interested me, and I became an international expert on several diseases, including haemolytic uremic syndrome and Henoch Schonlein purpura, but as the years went by, I realized that bedwetting was the problem that most interested me. This became very clear about twenty years ago. By that time, I had discovered that I could cure bedwetting in some children with a behavioural health therapy approach. In 1994, I published a paper on the success of my approach with a small group of patients.

Most paediatric kidney specialists spend the majority of their time helping children with chronic kidney failure. These children have very tough lives. You cannot cure their problem, and my job was mostly to ease their suffering along the way. I experienced lots of heartache working with these families. Some of these children even died while under my care.

Bedwetting, on the other hand, was not a life-threatening problem, and I had learned how to cure the problem in some children. Seeing the smile on the face of a child who was dry and who no longer needed to wear a pull-up at night was a very special occurrence that I enjoyed more and more. Around that time, I started to fantasize that one day, I might have a practice devoted exclusively to the care of children with bedwetting.

By 1996, I had published more than thirty papers on various aspects of bedwetting, and I was recognized internationally for my interest in this subject.

Time to write the book, I thought.

I wrote an outline, and after looking at the outline for several months and after several failed attempts to write the first page, I realized I really didn't know enough to write the book. There were still too many questions that I could not answer.

I continued to work as a paediatric nephrologist, but I spent more and more time thinking and writing about bedwetting, participating in international conferences on bedwetting, and speaking on bedwetting. I became a sought-after speaker on the subject, and I spoke at dozens of universities in the United States, Canada, and Europe. By the start of the new millennium, I had published more than sixty papers on bedwetting.

By 2003, I had decided that I really wanted to restrict my clinical work to bedwetting, and I accepted a position as professor of paediatric urology at the University of Oklahoma. Now, I am a nephrologist, not a urologist, so this requires an explanation.

A urologist is a surgeon who specializes in the kidney and the bladder. A nephrologist is a medical specialist of the kidney and the bladder. Some problems in the kidney and the bladder require a surgical solution, and some do not. For some problems, there are both surgical solutions and medical solutions, and there is a controversy about which approach is best. Medicine is a business, and surgeons and medical specialists often compete for patients with problems that could be treated with either a surgical or a medical approach. Competition, controversy, money, and medical egos are such that in many hospitals and universities, there exists an inbred animosity between the surgeons and the medical specialists.

I have always tried to bridge the gap between nephrology and urology, and I have enjoyed wonderful professional relationships with some of the most prominent paediatric urologists of the last half century. When I was offered the position of professor of paediatric urology, I considered this a great honour because this was proof that I had bridged a traditional gulf in the academic world.

My role in the department was to see all the bedwetting patients. This allowed the surgeons to focus on those problems that required surgery and allowed me to focus exclusively on my chosen field of interest.

I was definitely carving out an international presence in the area of bedwetting treatment. In 2004, I was invited to give a talk on bedwetting at the International Pediatric Nephrology Association (IPNA) Conference in Adelaide, Australia. The IPNA is *the* professional organization for my specialty. An invitation to present a review of a topic at this biannual conference was recognition by my nephrology peers that I knew what I was talking about. The American Academy of Pediatrics invited me to speak on bedwetting at their annual meeting in San Francisco in 2007 and again in 2010. At the most recent meeting, I was the chairperson of the session on bedwetting.

In 2006, I returned to Calgary to fulfill the dream and to start a clinic in my hometown to devote my energies exclusively to the care of children with bedwetting.

Over the last five years, I have seen more than a thousand children with bedwetting issues. I have helped all of them understand the problem, and I have cured more than 450 children. My dream came true!

In 2008, I was invited to write a review of bedwetting for the *New England Journal of Medicine* (*NEJM*). This is the most important and prestigious clinical journal in the world. An invitation to write a review for the *NEJM*, in my view, is something like an academic Academy Award. I could not believe my lucky stars. The paper came out in the spring of 2009, and my best friend had the issue framed for me.

In 2008, when I was invited to write the *NEJM* review, I tried again to write this book.

Surely now is the time, I thought.

I wrote a new outline, and I tried several times to start the book, but again, the words would not come. There was still something missing.

Over the last five years, I have had lots of "aha" moments when a piece of the bedwetting puzzle has come into focus. I continue to experience these moments, so I know I have not totally completed the puzzle.

However, recently, I have been able to predict with uncanny accuracy what a child or parent is going to say next in my office. The patterns seem very clear to me. When a child returns for a follow-up, I mostly know what that child will report. My work seems simpler now.

I expressed this sentiment to my eldest daughter.

"Daddy," she responded, "one of my professors at MIT told us that when we get to that point in our work when everything seems straightforward and simple, then it's time to write the book."

Two weeks later, I sat down, and the words flowed very naturally. I hope this book will be what makes the difference for a lot of families.

Acknowledgements

I have listened to the stories of thousands of parents and children, and we learn when we listen. Thank you to all those parents and children who have improved my understanding of this problem.

I have mentioned some of the famous physicians from whom I have learned over the years. There are many more whose names were not mentioned. Some of them are authors in the reference list. Thank you to all my colleagues.

Michele Holtsbaum, my medical assistant, suggested the name for the book. Thank you, Michele.

Josh Weaver solved the resolution problem with the ultrasound photos. Thank you, Josh.

I asked some parents to read the book and offer helpful comments. Many thanks to Monique P. and to the other parents for their great suggestions.

Kelli Taylor of KMT Solutions (kelli@kmtsolutions.ca) made a variety of helpful suggestions, and I recommend her to anyone who is in need of advice on editing.

Bobby

Bobby[1] is eight years old, and he just started grade three. When he grows up, he wants to play hockey in the NHL. He is an average student. The teacher reports he is sometimes a bit busy, but the school psychologist screened him for ADHD and she didn't think this was a concern. He sleeps for ten and a half hours, and Mom[2] wakes him at 7:00 a.m. on school days. His pull-up is heavy every morning, and several mornings a week, his bedsheets are also wet. Some weeks, the sheets are wet every morning. Mom doesn't say anything, but she is pretty tired of the extra laundry and has never felt good about the odour of urine when she walks into his room. Bobby pees in the toilet as soon as he gets up, and Mom cannot fathom how he could possibly still have any urine left in his body.

Breakfast on school days is usually one of the healthier cereals with about half a cup of milk. Mom encourages juice, but Bobby only eats his cereal and usually leaves an ounce or two of milk at the bottom of the bowl. Mom walks him to the bus stop at 7:40. The bus drops him at the school at 8:15, and he has some time to play with his pals before classes start. He has a granola bar or fruit gummy for a morning snack and a ham-and-cheese sandwich and chocolate milk for lunch. After gym, he stops for a drink at the water fountain, but so do all the boys. There is a bit of a rush, so the line moves fast and he doesn't drink much.

When he arrives home, he drops his pack inside the front door and races

---

1   Bedwetting is common in boys and girls, but more common in boys, so throughout this book, I will refer to Bobby as an example and use masculine pronouns for the child, but the same presentation applies to girls.

2   The most common person to accompany the child at the first visit to my office is the mother, so throughout this book, I will refer to the mother as the usual care person and use feminine pronouns, but of course, this could also be a father, other relative, or guardian.

to the bathroom. Mom can hear the pee and wishes Bobby would sit, because she knows that when he's in a rush and he stands, there will be quite a splatter on the seat and floor.

Mom sighs. "He's always in a rush." About half the days, his underwear is damp when he comes home; Mom can smell him.

He's getting better, though, she thinks. *I didn't need to send a change of clothes last year.*

Bobby always arrives home from school hungry and thirsty. Mom serves up some crackers and cheese, and he has a glass of juice. The house rule is that he cannot eat again until supper, but he can drink what he likes, and Bobby is back and forth several times to the water cooler before supper. At supper, Bobby often gets up from the supper table to pee, and Mom considers this a tactic to avoid eating his vegetables. He has a glass of milk at supper and often a glass of water as well. After supper, on at-home nights, Bobby has a bedtime snack of cereal with milk. He is always thirsty at bedtime, but Mom discourages anything more to drink. She knows he drinks some from the tap when he brushes his teeth, but she doesn't think he has more than a few ounces. On hockey nights, he drinks a lot more.

Mom has tried taking him to pee at 10:30 p.m., two hours after he falls asleep, but he is often already wet at that time, and he will still be wet the next morning if she changes his pull-up.

Bobby tried a bedwetting medication that the doctor prescribed to make him pee less at night, but he continued to wet even on the highest dose.

The family doctor keeps telling Mom not to worry, that bedwetting is normal at his age, and that he will outgrow the problem. Mom hopes this happens soon because Bobby has started to feel bad that he cannot go on sleepovers, and his younger brother, who is dry at night, sometimes teases him. Mom worries that the wetting might have an effect on his self-esteem and confidence.

Every day, I see two new children like Bobby in my office and six more children who return for follow-up at various stages of dryness.

Children wet the bed because their bladders do not hold as much pee as normal for their age or size. The kidneys make more pee overnight than the bladder can hold, and at the moment when the bladder is full, the child does not wake up. This straightforward set of circumstances is present in almost every elementary school–aged child who wets the bed.

The basic causes of bedwetting are remarkably consistent. How these causes evolve, however, is different in every child and family, even when bedwetting happens in siblings.

The cure for bedwetting requires a treatment approach that addresses all three causes of the problem.

1.   The bladder needs to hold more.
2.   The kidney needs to make less pee than the bladder can hold.
3.   The child needs to wake up before the full bladder empties.

Success with behavioural health therapy requires three things.

1.   The parent—and hopefully the child too, if old enough—must understand why the behaviour needs to be changed.
2.   The parent or child must have a good reason to change the behaviour.
3.   Finally, the parent and child must have the necessary time and discipline to work on the recommendations.

Understanding why the behaviour needs to be changed is very important. This is why I spend two hours with the child and family during the initial visit at my office and an hour with each follow-up visit. These visits are teaching sessions. I need to explain the situation in a way that makes sense to the parents and the child. When I see the light of understanding in their eyes, this makes all the difference.

Most parents are motivated, and they presume that their child is motivated as well, but this is not always the case. Many bedwetting specialists teach that you should not offer therapy until the child is motivated. While this is a good general rule, I am happy to start therapy as long as the child will be compliant.

Time and discipline are the biggest obstacles to success. My approach sounds so simple, and indeed is simple in theory, but in practice, the challenges can be daunting. I discuss this carefully in later chapters.

When a child does not improve with my recommendations, this is certainly not the fault of the child. Mostly this is because either the child or the family is not ready for this intervention. Many children do not succeed the first time, but they do when they return a year or two later.

I had a mom come in recently who got mad at me right away. She and her daughter had tried my approach a few years before but without success.

"I'm just here to get a medication," she demanded.

A decade ago, I would likely have pulled out my prescription pad and written out a script for a medication.

I let the mom vent her frustrations and feelings, and this lasted about ten or fifteen minutes. The daughter sat quietly.

Once Mom paused, I asked some questions to determine the current situation. I discovered that the child had improved more than the mother had realized; the daughter was able to give me some examples that suggested that her bladder held more now than it did two years ago. I pointed this out to Mom. The bladder was holding more in part because the child was older, but mostly because the child had continued to work on my basic bowel health recommendations.

I advised Mom that while the medication might well work, this approach would only be a control and not a cure. I added that the daughter would likely need to stay on the medication for several years, and I discussed the side effects of the medication.

By the halfway point in the visit, the mother had settled down, and she was listening well to my pep talk about how things would be different this time. I convinced her to give my recommendations another try. Six months later, her daughter was totally dry. This sort of outcome makes my day.

The first chapters of this book will discuss why children don't wake up to pee, why bladders don't hold enough, and why kidneys make more pee than the bladder can hold. The subsequent chapters will outline my treatment approach; I will tell you what you need to do to cure the bedwetting in your child. This approach will work whether your child is six or sixteen.

Why Don't Children Wake Up to Pee?

Almost all parents tell me that their child wets the bed because he sleeps "too deeply," "so soundly," or "hard." This universal sense of the cause is intuitive to a parent. A mom understands that if she drinks too much in the evening, then she will need to wake up to pee. She knows that she can wake up to go to the bathroom if she needs to, and she also realizes that her child can't. The obvious conclusion is that bedwetting is due to a sleep pattern that is so deep that the child cannot wake up.

This is certainly part of the problem.

However, lots of children sleep just as deeply and would not wake up if they had a full bladder, but these children don't wet the bed. A European study[3] reported that 30 per cent of seven-year-old to twelve-year-old children who were given enough water at bedtime to fill the bladder overnight did not wake up and wet the bed. None of these children had ever wet the bed before. Presumably, these children either have an adequate-sized bladder or their kidneys do not produce more urine overnight than their bladder could hold.

Conversely, about 10 per cent of ten-year-old children routinely wake up to pee every night. If these children did not wake up, they would wet the bed. Presumably, these children have a bladder that does not hold enough relative to how much urine their kidneys make overnight.

Why children who wet the bed do not wake up is not well understood. I have my own theory, which I will share later in the book. We know much more about why a bladder doesn't hold as much and why the kidney makes so much pee overnight.

What is understood about sleep is that right from birth, children

---

3   J. Kirk, P. V. Rasmussen, S. Rittig, et al., "Provoked Enuresis-like Episodes in Healthy Children 7 to 12 Years Old," *Journal of Urology* 156 (1996): 210–13.

experience a partial arousal before they empty the bladder. This was shown in a simple, but absolutely brilliant, sentinel study[4] by Dr. C. K. Yeung, one of the foremost experts on bedwetting in the world. I was in Aarhus, Denmark, in 1995 when C. K. reported his findings at an international conference. I'd never met C. K., but I had read some of his papers. He trained at Great Ormond Street in London, England, and had recently returned to Hong Kong to start his career. Until he published this important research, the conventional wisdom of the day was that infants emptied their bladder because of a spinal reflex. That is, when the bladder reached full, a nerve message traveled from the bladder to the lower spinal cord, and this generated a reflex return message from the spinal cord to relax the sphincter muscle that holds the pee in.

This mistaken understanding was one of the main reasons why bedwetting was considered to be a "developmental" problem. Proponents of the "developmental" cause presumed that this reflex persisted in children who wet the bed and that these children had not yet developed the control that comes from the brain.

I never believed the developmental cause theory even before C. K.'s research. Children who wet the bed clearly demonstrate control from the brain during the day. I didn't believe that the brain would have normal control by day but not have control at night.

When C. K. proved that newborn infants experience a partial arousal before emptying the bladder, he provided proof that the spinal reflex theory was not valid. There are still many physicians who believe and teach that bedwetting is a "developmental" problem, and in my view, these people are simply wrong. Not only are these physicians wrong, but by using the word *developmental* when they speak to parents and children, they bring to mind ideas and thoughts that the child might have delayed development, which to many parents has wider implications.

C. K. has a reputation as a person who can get by without much sleep, and this was how he managed to do his research. While at Great Ormand Street, he worked his usual very busy clinical day, and then he stayed up all night to watch newborn infants sleep. The diapers were continuously monitored for urine by both videotapes and C. K.'s own observations, which confirmed that there was an arousal prior to each void.

After his Aarhus presentation, I introduced myself to C. K. and congratulated him on his brilliant research. I added, "I know why the babies wake up before they pee."

C. K. looked very serious, as if somehow I knew something that he didn't.

---

4   C. K. Yeung, M. L. Godley, C. K. W. Ho, et al., "Some New Insights into Bladder Function in Infancy," *BJU* 76 (1995): 235–40.

I laughed and went on, "Of course they woke up. They wanted to let their mothers know so that their diapers could be changed."

We both laughed, and we have been professional friends ever since.

What I was actually thinking about at that time was the story I'd heard about a West African culture where the children are reported to be "toilet trained" by one year of age. These infants sleep in the same bed with their mothers. At the first signs of arousal, the mother takes her child to a toilet area. This practice has apparently been handed down for generations, and these children are dry at night from a much earlier age than occurs in North America or Europe.

Arousal has not been studied very much in children who wet the bed. However, what is clear is that partial arousals are common in children who wet the bed and that children who wet the bed continue to experience a partial arousal before the bladder empties. The partial arousal might manifest as restless sleep or talking in the sleep. Some children open and close their eyes or sit up. A few sleepwalk. The child remembers none of this, but a small per cent of parents are observant enough to report the relationship between a partial arousal and bedwetting. These mothers have been up otherwise, perhaps with a younger sibling or to pee, and over time, they have learned that the partial arousal immediately precedes the bedwetting. The most common story from these mothers is that when they heard their child talking or being restless, they checked on the child and noted that the pull-up was not only wet but also warm. The child had just peed. Some of these mothers take their child to pee during the partial arousals, and in the treatment chapter on alarm therapy, we will learn that this makes good sense.

Lots of parents relate stories of sleepwalking children who pee in unusual locations, places other than in the toilet. The most common locations are in the bathroom, just not in the toilet. The parent finds the pee puddle the next morning. Other common locations include hallways and potted plants. These children and their parents often report the sleepwalking stories as humorous anecdotes, which is a healthy and positive perspective.

Some children sleepwalk and do pee in the toilet. This is likely more common than many parents appreciate. Typically, the parent hears the child get out of bed, walk to the bathroom, and pee in the toilet, or the next morning, the parent finds the bathroom light on or the toilet not flushed. The parents presume the child was awake. However, many of these children have absolutely no recollection of getting up and peeing. They were sleepwalking during the partial arousal that would otherwise have preceded an episode of bedwetting.

I believe that a full bladder might trigger some episodes of night terror,[5] and I have helped some parents to successfully interrupt a night terror by taking their child to pee.

Some children do wake up with a full bladder in the middle of the night, but they do not get out of bed and pee.

I suspect that some children wake up but do not recognize that a full bladder was the reason why they woke up. The child might open his eyes, move around under the covers, reposition his pillow, and fall back asleep without ever making the connection that his bladder was full. A full bladder signal lying down in bed is different than a full bladder signal perceived when the child is awake and walking around. Many children learn to postpone voiding and hold their pee during the day, and this blurs the daytime perception of the early signal of a full bladder. At night, the child cannot postpone voiding, and the early signal is likely quite different in intensity compared to the day signal.

Other children do recognize that the bladder is full, but they might be reluctant to get out of bed and go to the bathroom. From the perspective of a child, there are many reasons not to get out of bed. The room is dark. Who knows what might lurk in their imagination along the dark corridor to the bathroom? These are common fears in a toddler, and I suspect that some prefer to pee in their diaper rather than brave the journey.

When I was about four or five years of age, I was frightened about what might live under my bed. When I woke up in the morning, I would stand on the bed and jump several feet clear. I would certainly never let my feet dangle over the bed. Had I awakened with a full bladder in the middle of the night, I'm not sure I would have braved the jump into the darkness.

If a child chooses not to get out of bed to pee when he wakes up to the signal of a full bladder, and if the child does this repeatedly, perhaps this is part of the problem. The brain responds to all of our actions and learns. In this situation, the brain might learn that a child prefers to wet in the diaper rather than to get up to pee, so the brain allows the signal to wake up to become a form of background noise, and over time, the child might lose the ability to respond to the signal of a full bladder at night.

There are other reasons apart from imaginary monsters that might dissuade a child from getting out of bed. The room might be cold. Who really wants to get out of a warm and cozy bed? A child who sleeps in a top bunk is much less likely to get up to pee.

Many children wake up and go to their mother. I teach mothers that

5   Night terrors are not nightmares. During a night terror, the child might have his eyes open, but he is not aware of the presence of his parent and has no recollection of the episode the following morning.

every time a child comes to them in the middle of the night, the child should be instructed to pee before he either snuggles up in Mom's bed or before he goes back to his own bed.

Children at the age of five years sleep an average of eleven hours a night. The duration of sleep falls slowly each year so that by the age of sixteen years, the average is eight and a half hours. One of the reasons why a child "naturally outgrows" the bedwetting is that the duration of sleep falls over time, and there is progressively less time for the bladder to fill up.

Below is a table that shows the average duration of sleep by age.

Age (years)	Average Duration of Sleep (hours)
1	13¾
2	13
3	12
4	11½
5	11
6	10¾
7	10½
8	10¼
9	10
10	9¾
11	9½
12	9¼
13	9¼
14	9
15	8¾
16	8½
17	8¼
18	8¼

There are four stages of sleep, and the percentage of time spent in the deeper stages is higher in the first half of the sleep cycle. The percentage of time spent in deeper sleep gets less through the night. I have noted that children are able to wake up to pee more easily during the last half of the sleep cycle than during the first half. How much the bladder holds and how fast the kidney makes pee overnight are the factors that determine when a bladder will become full during the sleep cycle. The less the bladder holds and the faster the kidneys make pee in the first few hours after a child falls asleep, the more likely the bladder will fill during the first half of the sleep cycle when it is harder to wake up.

While I was at the University of Oklahoma, I published a study on the differences between children who had always wet the bed (primary-onset bedwetting) and children who were consistently dry for a period of time before the wetting started (secondary-onset bedwetting). I was very pleased when the paper was accepted in *Pediatrics*, the journal of the American Pediatric Society, because papers need to be of very high quality to be accepted in this journal. I reported that there were no major differences between these two groups of children with bedwetting. This implies that the causes are the same.

About a quarter of children who wet the bed have secondary-onset bedwetting. Before the bedwetting started, most of these children did not need to wake up to pee to stay dry; they just slept dry. Presumably, at that time, these children had a bladder that held enough for the amount of urine the kidneys made overnight. These children started to wet because something changed and either their bladder could no longer hold as much or their kidneys made more pee than the bladders could hold. I believe the most likely initiating event is a change in how much the bladder will hold.

A smaller per cent of the children with secondary-onset bedwetting were dry before the bedwetting started because they woke up to pee one or more times overnight. Presumably, these children already had bladders that did not hold enough to accommodate the amount of urine the kidneys made overnight. Perhaps what happened to these children was that the bladder started to hold even less or that the rate of urine production immediately after sleep was higher such that the bladder filled up earlier in the sleep cycle, when it is harder for a child to wake up. Another possibility is that something fundamental to the arousal process changed.

Peeing in a diaper is too easy. If parents notice that their toddler can wake up to pee in the middle of the night, I encourage a nightlight in the room and a nightlight in the corridor. When a child can wake up to pee, this is a good time to take the child out of the diaper. If a child has achieved dryness at night because he routinely wakes up to pee, and if this child starts to wet again, I do not recommend putting the child back in a diaper. As soon as this happens, the main priority should be to improve the bowel health, because this is likely the reason why the bladder is holding less and therefore emptying earlier in the sleep cycle. This will be discussed in the chapter on bladder-friendly bowel health, "Why Do Bladders Act Small?" I believe that early intervention in children with secondary-onset bedwetting can lead to a prompt return to dryness. Once the pattern of wetting becomes well established, a prompt return to dryness is usually not possible.

Why Do Bladders Act Small?

The bladder is a muscular sac at the bottom of the pelvis. The two tubes (ureters) that carry the urine from each kidney enter on the same side behind and below the bladder. The tube (urethra) that the pee comes out of is in the middle at the bottom of the bladder. There is a sphincter muscle wrapped around the first part of this tube, and this muscle is meant to be tight all the time and only relax when we want the pee to come out. The sphincter muscle is the reason we don't leak all the time.

The pelvis of a child is small, and the bones of the pelvis are rigid. The pelvis forms a boney funnel, and there is very little room at the bottom of the pelvis. The bowel comes down the left side of the abdomen and is cheek-to-jowl with the bladder at the bottom of the pelvis. The rectum is right alongside the bladder. The bladder and bowel are in a very intimate relationship; a full bladder pushes on the rectum, and a full rectum pushes on the bladder.

Pregnant women understand about pressure on the bladder. The baby in their womb causes pressure on the bladder, and as the baby grows and takes up progressively more space in the pelvis, the mother needs to pee more often during the day and needs to get up at night to pee.

The pressure of poop causes a similar situation in the pelvis of a small child. The most common reason why a bladder does not hold enough urine is the effect of poop pressing on the bladder.

I teach parents that it is not a question of whether the poop is pressing on the bladder, but rather, in their child, how much of an impact this makes on the size of the bladder.

Some children who come to my office for the first visit have constipation that is already under treatment or that has been treated in the past. Some children have longstanding constipation that has not been recognized. However, most of the children who come to my office do not fit with the diagnostic criteria for constipation. These children might not have constipation per se, but neither do they have what I call "bladder-friendly bowel health." Improving the bowel health is necessary to cure bedwetting.

Bladder-Friendly Bowel Health

Hard and pasty poop forms what I call a "poop wall" around the bladder. The bladder muscles are precisely designed to push liquid pee out though a tube. The bladder muscles cannot push solid poop away. The poop wall compromises the capacity of the bladder, and this wall is also the most common reason why children need to run to the bathroom and why children wet during the day. Once the bladder has reached full and is therefore up against the poop wall, the bladder cannot push the poop out of the way. When the bladder is up against the poop wall, the child must respond promptly to that signal of full, or in due course, there will be a race to the bathroom and varying degrees of dampness or wetting.

Below are ultrasound images of the poop wall in a nine and a quarter-year-old boy who wet the bed every night and more than once a night. The skin surface of the abdomen is on the top. The dark black area is the bladder filled with urine. The oval, grey-and-white area is poop in the rectum below the bladder. Note in the image on the left how the hard poop in the rectum is pushing into the bladder. When the poop is pushing into the bladder, the bladder is frowning. ☹ The distance between the two points marked by the number 1 is 45 millimetres (almost two inches). A normal distance should be half that, or about 20 to 25 millimetres. Below on the right is an ultrasound image from the same child taken at the same time as the image above, but this is the lateral view. Notice how the hard poop in the rectum has squished the bladder up against the tummy wall.

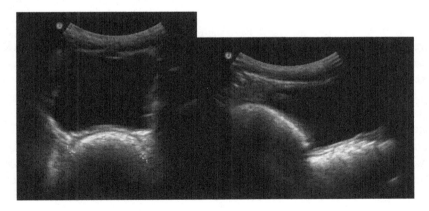

Below are ultrasound images of the same child, but these are images after the family worked on my recommendations, and these images show bladder-friendly bowel health. Note that the bladder in the image on the left has a nice curved shape. The poop is not pushing into the bladder. When the poop is not pushing into the bladder, the bladder is smiling. ☺ Note also that the diameter of the rectum under the bladder—the distance between the two points marked by the number 1—is now 26 millimetres, much improved and in the normal range. The image on the right is the lateral view of the above-mentioned image. Compare this to the lateral view image on the last page. The bladder can now push the soft poop out of the way. The second set of images was taken seven months after the first set, and at that time, the boy had been consistently dry at night for one month.

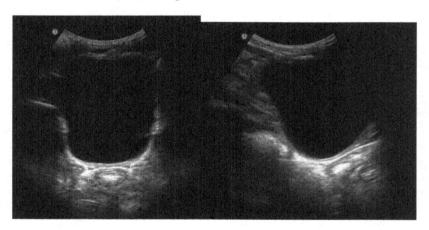

The race to the bathroom is called "urgency", and about three-quarters of the children I see with bedwetting have urgency and at least minor pre-void dampness on a regular basis and often every day. Those who don't have these symptoms are often older, and these symptoms were usually a feature of their voiding when they were younger. A very common history is for children to continue to need to run to the bathroom through elementary school, but for the running to slowly become less and less common with each new grade. These children often have regular daytime wetting sufficient to change the clothes through kindergarten and into grade one, but this amount of wetting becomes progressively less common and usually disappears by about grade three. The minor pre-void daytime dampness often continues as long as there is urgency. Most mothers are not aware that their children continue to leak a tiny amount before they make it to the bathroom. Small urine stains are routinely missed in the underwear, especially if the underwear is not white.

Many mothers presume the small urine stains they see in the underwear when they do the laundry are due to urine that comes out after the children pee.

In my experience, only about 10 or 20 per cent of children who wet the bed have never had problems with urgency and daytime dampness; these children usually have a personality that is very attentive to bladder signals. They void frequently enough to prevent dampness because for them, even minor dampness is not an acceptable option. I will discuss these children in more detail in a subsequent chapter.

As bowel health improves in the children who follow my recommendations, the urgency and dampness become less and less, and for most parents and children, the improved daytime control is a very welcome sign of progress.

Breast-fed infants usually poop more than once a day and often after each feeding. Our bodies are built to poop after meals. As soon as food stretches the stomach, there is a signal sent to the bowel to push the poop along and to empty if there is poop in the rectum. This is called the gastro-colic reflex (stomach-colon reflex), and this makes good sense. When we eat, we need to empty below to make room for the new food, which in due course will become poop. When children get up from a meal to pee, they are really responding to the bowel signal. The poop in the bowel is pushed down into the rectum, and the poop bumps into the bladder. The increased pressure on the bladder makes the child want to pee. These children are not avoiding their vegetables. Ideally, these children would pee and poop at this time. However, this is uncommon. If you ask these children whether they feel as if they need to poop when they get up from the supper table, most will indicate they do not recognize the poop signal at all. At that time, the pee signal is the strongest signal. Once a child empties the bladder, there is more room for the poop and the poop signal (pressure in the rectum) is less prominent. The signal then is either ignored or fades away. A small per cent of these children do recognize the poop signal, and they sit to poop at that time. Other children recognize the poop signal, but they are not prepared to respond to the signal and poop during dinner, perhaps because they will take too long and their dinner will get cold or their parents might complain, or perhaps because pooping and then eating is "gross."

Optimally, what we eat today should be pooped out tomorrow. This is what happens in breast-fed infants who poop multiple times a day. They have terrific transit time. The transit time is the time it takes for food to move from the mouth to the toilet. There are very few children who wet the bed and have a good transit time. Even if a child poops every day, the transit time is usually slow because most of the children don't empty well when they do poop. Most don't poop every day, and they also don't empty well. That is a double whammy. These children build solid perpetual poop walls around their bladders.

You can test the transit time in your child. Offer fresh corn for supper one night, and then check the poop each day until you see empty corn kernels in the poop.

Emptying is a major culprit in the story of bedwetting.

When a breast-fed infant poops multiple times a day with the typical seedy yellow poops, the mom knows about the poop because she can hear the poop gurgle out or because she knows to check and does. These children don't need to push, and they don't get red in the face, grimace, or look uncomfortable when they poop.

Somewhere along the way, the poop starts to firm up. There are numerous common reasons why poop firms up. Dietary changes are common causes and include supplementation with a formula, adding solids, and weaning to cow's milk.

Anything that causes an infant to get dehydrated will lead to firmer poop. This can happen during an illness when an infant doesn't feed as well or when vomiting and diarrhoea develop. Everyone loses water with every breath because the air in our lungs is moist. The water lost from the lungs is increased in dry climates and during respiratory illnesses. The skin is a common source of water loss, and the ratio of skin surface to body volume of an infant or child is relatively much greater than that of an adult. Infants dehydrate more quickly with fevers and when the ambient temperature is very high. I've noted that constipation can start during hot summers, when infants are outside a lot or on tropical winter vacations.

As soon as the poop firms up, there comes a time when the infants or children experience some difficulty or discomfort as they pass the poop.

"Ouch," they feel. "I don't like that. Next time that poop comes along, I'm going to say, 'No, thank you,' and I'm not going to let that poop come out. I'm going to hold that poop in."

And they do, and they can do this from the first week of life. They do not do this consciously. I think they do this as a natural response to discomfort.

When this happens, they start to build the poop wall.

Withholding is what perpetuates the bowel problem.

Parents often tell me that they thought all babies pushed to poop. Some parents tell stories of how their child strained, got red in the face, and grimaced, and some even tell these stories as if these expressions and postures were somehow funny. I don't get it. There is nothing funny about discomfort and pain.

There are a variety of postures that children use to withhold the poop. Children might squeeze their bum cheeks together, cross their legs, squeeze

16

their thighs together, arch their backs, or hold on to a piece of furniture to brace themselves. Parents often presume these postures are because the child is trying to poop, but mostly these postures are because the child is trying to hold the poop in and not poop.

If the poop is soft enough, infants don't need to push. Not only does hard and pasty poop not empty well, but the pushing per se also interferes with emptying. The children push some poop out, but when the abdominal and pelvic floor muscles tense up with the push, the poop is "cut off," and while a portion is pushed out, the remaining portion is pushed back in. Unless a child sits patiently and waits for the remaining poop to settle back down, he will not empty. Most children presume they have emptied and carry on with their play.

Recently, I watched a movie where one of the bad guys had a bathroom problem; he either went to the bathroom or talked about going to the bathroom in numerous scenes. The scriptwriter must like toilet humour. In one scene, the fellow asked his partners to wait for him while he "pinched off a loaf." This pretty accurately describes how the poop is "cut" off with pushing. A loaf doesn't sound skinny, does it?

Pooping in a diaper is "child's play" compared to pooping on a toilet. Children who walk around in a diaper can achieve the natural squat to empty the bowel. The squat is how the body was meant to empty. Before there were bathrooms, people walked out to the designated poop place, positioned their feet shoulder-width apart and flat on the ground, allowed their knees to come apart as the bum descended, and while so positioned, the poop and the pee came out. For pregnant women, this was also the birthing posture. This is the posture that naturally relaxes the pelvic floor muscles, which are the muscles around the bum hole. As the pelvic floor muscles relax, emptying is improved.

Toilets are a modern sanitary convenience, and they were designed for adult bums and legs. Infant and preschool children cannot empty well on an adult toilet without an over-the-toilet seat, a footstool, and instruction on how to properly sit and relax. Most children perch forward with their knees together, tottering on the brink of the seat. Some hold themselves up over the middle of the toilet with their hands on the sides of the toilet seat. Without attention to proper posture, emptying is compromised.

While travelling in Europe, I came across this medieval castle bathroom. The small wooden potty at the end confirms they understood about posture centuries ago.

The modern North American toilet was invented in Victorian-era England. The room with the toilet was called a water closet, or WC, because this was a small room where you passed water. I have heard people remark that one of the greatest achievements of the British Empire, which peaked under Victoria's reign, was the export of modern plumbing. I don't agree.

Modern Victorian-era plumbing did not catch on outside of the empire. I recollect my first experience with the alternative toilet solution. I was twenty-two years old. I had just finished medical school, and I was backpacking in Europe. The toilets in France, which was my first stop after England, were two concrete footpads on either side of a hole. Since I was brought up to expect the porcelain throne, these toilets were offensive. Since then, I have learned that the footpads-beside-the-hole solution continues to be the norm in many parts of Asia and the Middle East. These cultures have developed modern systems that are both sanitary and allow the natural posture to poop.

Of course, most of the people in the world do not enjoy the luxury of any plumbing. They just squat in the designated poop place. The full body-length tunic worn by so many different cultures is practical because the garment can be easily pulled up and kept off the ground when the child squats to poop.

Right or wrong, Victorian-era plumbing did catch on in North America, and parents need to work around this invention to achieve bladder-friendly bowel health.

Lots of parents start off toilet training with a floor potty, and posture can be quite good in this situation. However, few parents enjoy transferring the pee and poop into the toilet and the cleaning up that is required, and most parents therefore encourage transition to the adult toilet within a few months.

When parents encourage toilet training, they often sit their child on the toilet to practice. Some children with hard, pasty poop cooperate fine to pee in the toilet, but they refuse to make the transition for poop. Hard, pasty poop that

This is an example of plumbing in Japan that allows the natural squat.

doesn't empty well is likely the most common reason why children poop on the toilet later than they pee on the toilet. These children know that pooping is easier in a pull-up than on the toilet. They intuitively know better than their parents, but they don't have the words to tell them.

Some children wear underwear by day, and these children will pee in the toilet and stay dry, but they ask their parents for a pull-up to poop. This drives some parents crazy because they cannot figure out why the child will pee but not poop in the toilet. Parents are usually happy to accept this as a reasonable compromise so that the child can wear underwear by day. Many of these mothers send their child to preschool, day care, or kindergarten in underwear. The child holds in the poop all day, and as soon as he gets home, he asks his mother for a pull-up.

Rarely, I come across some very bright children who figure out a way to comply with their parents' request to use the adult toilet and also to achieve the correct posture. These children stand on the toilet seat and squat over the hole. Amazing ingenuity! I don't recommend this because squatting over the hole is also an acrobatic achievement that might not be possible for every child.

So far, we have learned that poop firms up for a variety of common reasons, and as soon as this happens, the child learns that he can withhold the poop, and he does. The pattern changes from a normal daily morning poop routine to a random pattern and then to days without a poop. Since the poop is firmer, the emptying is compromised. With toilet training and the transition to the adult toilet, the emptying is further compromised.

The average age of toilet training in North America is about two and a half years. Some children achieve this milestone at one and a half years and others at three and a half years. Success between these ages is considered acceptable.

During this time, some other important events are usually happening in the world of the child. Some mothers go back to work, and children start to attend day cares and preschools. By about the age of three years, children develop a social sense of bathrooms. They are comfortable with their mother wiping their bottom after a poop; they are familiar with the bathrooms in their own home; and they have learned that poop and bathrooms are generally considered dirty. Once three-year-olds leave home during the day, they will usually hold their poop until they come home and their mother is available to wipe. Leaving home for any reason increases withholding.

Most families are rushed in the morning. In the space of an hour, and often less, two parents and one or more children need to wake up, dress, eat, and leave the house, often to a different location for each individual. Pooping in the morning, which was the natural time to poop for most infants, now becomes a rare event during the week and might only happen on weekends.

Once a toddler leaves home to a day care or school reality, the pattern of

In 1996, I attended the International Continence Society meetings in Athens, Greece. My daughter attended with me, and while we were looking around in the Acropolis Museum, we came across a terra cotta potty from several thousand years ago. The height is not optimal for the heels to be flat. The pee hole for little boys is cute.

pooping falls below the radar of the mother. Most mothers presume the child is pooping outside the home, but this is usually not the case.

Prior to the first visit to my office, I ask the mothers to download some questionnaires on voiding and pooping and to answer the questions before the visit. I want the mothers to start thinking about some of the questions I will ask. Mothers are requested to circle the number of days each week that their child has a poop. They can circle numbers 1 to 7. More than 75 per cent of mothers report that their child poops every day.

I take a pee and poop history directly from every child who is six years of age or older and from some more mature five-year-olds. I tell the child that he is a big boy, that the answers are easy, and that there is no rush to answer. Then I tell the child that the rule is that the child needs to answer without any help from the mother. In my experience, about 10 per cent of mothers find this rule impossible to follow and try to answer for their child.

My first question about poop is, "Do you poop every day, or are there days that you don't poop?"

I never look at the mother. I keep the child's attention focused on me.

Almost every child answers, "I don't poop every day."

I ask the next question.

"Some boys only go one day without a poop, but others go two days, some three, some four, some even go longer without a poop. How many days do you think you have ever gone without a poop?"

When the answer is multiple days, many mothers refuse to believe their child, but I believe him.

Many children only poop every other day. An alternate-day pattern looks like a daily pattern to most busy mothers. And remember, not only do they not poop on many days, but also when they do poop, they don't empty well.

Some children only poop on weekends. I call them "weekend poopers." Some of these children are so busy during the week that they do not have enough home time that coincides with the signals to achieve a Monday-to-Friday poop. These children commonly are rushed out of the home thirty to forty-five minutes after they wake up, are on school buses before and after school, attend preschool and after-school care, or are enrolled in multiple sport, dance, or music activities.

Most parents presume that "skid marks" in the underwear are a wiping problem. In my office, skid marks are usually minor soilings,[6] and this is a major clue to the presence of poor bowel health. I have parents who deny that their child soils, but during the exam, I find a teaspoon or a tablespoon of poop between the cheeks. These mothers are clearly in denial.

Some parents acknowledge that their child did have problems with constipation during infancy or the toddler years. When I hear this, I know the child is still missing days, that his poop is pasty, and that he doesn't empty well. These mothers are often easier to convince about the bowel health issues.

Some mothers insist that their child does not have a bowel issue. They deny what their child reports, and they often rely on the "I wipe his bum and I know" defence.

---

6   Soiling in this book refers only to poop accidents and not to pee accidents. The medical term for soiling is *encopresis*.

21

Other mothers agree that the child doesn't poop every day but deny this is a concern.

"She has normal bowel health; she poops every other day, just like me."

Some mothers ask me, "Is it normal to poop every day?" OMG, yes!

There are a variety of notions about what is normal for bowel health. For the record, I teach that bladder-friendly bowel health is the best bowel health. This means a poop every morning after breakfast before the child starts either the school or play day, great emptying when the child poops, and soft mushy poop that breaks apart and does not keep the log shape. Children who poop every morning can also poop a second time every day, and some can even poop three times.

You cannot poop too often if you want a big bladder.

There is an Oprah story about what constitutes normal poop. Apparently, there was a doctor on her talk show who taught that normal poop is a pasty log with an S shape. I don't agree. Our poop should be softer and should not keep the shape when flushed away.

Missing days is certainly common in children, as is wide, pasty poop and the need to push, but common is not the same as normal. I do not consider a poop wall, a compromised bladder capacity, and bedwetting to be normal.

There are other reasons why a bladder does not hold a normal amount. Bladder infection is the next most common reason. Bladder infection is much more common in girls than boys and should be checked for in every child with bedwetting. The most common symptoms of bladder infection are discomfort with voiding, bad-smelling urine, and day and night wetting. Some children have no symptoms at all; they just have an infection. A later chapter will address the causes, treatment, and prevention of bladder infection.

Bowel health and bladder infection are the two most common reasons why a bladder does not hold enough urine. Achieving dryness means that there must be no infection on the inside of the bladder and no poop wall outside the bladder.

A rare cause of a bladder that does not hold a normal amount is a nerve problem from the spine to the bladder. The most common cause of this is spina bifida (myelomeningocele). These children are born with a congenital defect in the lower spine. Nerve problems can also develop in children who have a spinal injury (from diving, trampolines, motor vehicle accidents, falls). Very rarely, a child develops a tumour or cyst in the spinal canal, and the pressure on the nerves to the bladder can cause the bladder to act small. Collectively, all spinal causes are referred to as a neurogenic bladder.

Another rare cause of a bladder that does not hold the normal amount is a blockage in the tube (urethra) that comes out of the bladder. This is called a posterior urethral valve. This is always in boys and is usually picked up during a prenatal ultrasound.

There is no such thing as a congenitally small bladder. Children are not born with a small bladder, and they do not inherit a small bladder. The bladders of all the children I see with bowel health and infection issues are only "acting small." With treatment and time, these bladders can act a normal size.

There is one other very rare cause of bedwetting, and although this is not necessarily associated with a bladder that doesn't hold enough, this is probably the best time to mention this problem. Sometimes, the ureter, the tube from the kidney, can bypass the bladder and connect directly to the outside. This is called an ectopic ureter and is a rare congenital problem that happens almost exclusively in girls. Since there is no sphincter to hold the pee in, the urine from that kidney continuously leaks out. The key feature of these girls is that they are "always wet"; every time the mother checks the underwear, even if she checks every fifteen minutes, there will always be dampness.

During the first visit to my clinic, one of the most important goals is to establish how much the bladder of the child can hold in a relaxed fashion. I want to clarify the volume when the child is full. I know the bladder will not hold as much as normal; I want to know how small is small for that child.

I accomplish this by asking the child to drink sufficient fluids to be able to pee at least twice during the visit. I ask the child to tell me when he needs to pee, and I clarify that the child should tell me without any prompting from the parent. The child is instructed to tell me as soon as he feels full. I define full as how he might feel when he is at home, not doing anything special, and the bathroom is close by. In other words, there is no good reason for him not to pee. My exam room is set up such that I sit across from the child and the mother sits to the left. I mostly speak to the child, and I am constantly watching for the telltale posture signs of an overfull bladder. Either when the child tells me he is full or when I am sure he is displaying typical posturing, I take the child into my ultrasound room and do a pelvic ultrasound. I identify the full bladder and the rectum. I assess the effect of the poop on the shape of the bladder, and I measure the diameter of the rectum under the full bladder. Then I ask the child to go to another room to pee in a special toilet (Uroflow) that measures aspects of bladder function and the amount of urine that comes out. For girls and for boys who routinely sit to pee, I specifically counsel the children on the correct posture to pee. For boys who stand to pee, I review the importance of pulling the pants or zipper all the way down so that the penis is not bent while the pee comes out. After he pees, the child is instructed to return immediately (he is not even allowed to wash his hands) to the ultrasound room for a post-void image. I measure how much pee is left in the bladder; I measure the diameter of the rectum under the empty bladder; and I measure the thickness of the bladder wall.

The special Uroflow toilet generates a pee curve, which shows how the urine flowed out of the bladder. A normal pee curve is a bell shape. The Uroflow also measures how much pee came out.

I define a bladder as full when the child tells me he needs to pee without any evidence of posturing, when the bladder empties completely on the post-void image, and when the shape of the pee curve is a bell shape. When a bladder is overfull, the child might be posturing, the bladder does not empty, and the pee curve becomes broader. As a bladder becomes progressively more overfull, the child postures more, the amount of urine left in the bladder increases, and the pee curve becomes progressively broader.

I point out to the child and the parents that while a child can purposefully hold his pee in the bladder past the signal of full by day, he cannot do this while he is asleep. There is no conscious control in a bedwetting child when he is asleep.

If the child has voided with an overfull bladder despite my best efforts to encourage voiding at the first signal, I ask the child to tell me "sooner" with the next void, and he continues to drink and pee until either we identify the correct value of full or the time runs out for the visit. Two hours is booked for each first visit, and during this time, I am able to get a good sense of what is full for almost every child.

I plot the value of full for the child on a graph that shows what the bladder should hold by age, and this illustrates the extent of the problem to the parent. Some are amazed at how little the bladder holds. I commonly see values of only a few ounces in elementary school–aged children. Parents who read this book should plot how much their child pees on the graph. The first graph has the capacity in ounces, and the second graph has the capacity in millilitres.

Average Bladder Capacity by Age

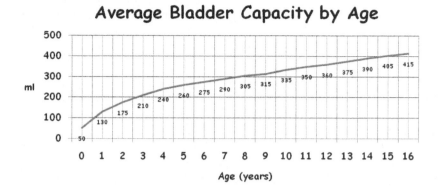

Average Bladder Capacity by Age

Parents don't have a Uroflow to check the pee curve, and they don't have an ultrasound to assess how well the bladder emptied, but they can measure how much the child pees on those occasions when he feels the need to pee (full) but is not running to the bathroom. For children who tend to hold the pee, this volume will almost always be higher than the relaxed full volume, but for those children who are attentive voiders, this will be a good estimate.

You would think that all children with a bladder that acts small would need to pee frequently, but this is not so. Some children pee as often as ten or more times a day, while others with a bladder capacity that is just as small pee only three times a day. Many children pee the average number of times a day, which is four to six.

After drinking a larger than usual amount of juice or water, these children need to pee frequently. The small size of their bladder is often only evident after a big drink of juice or water.

Parents and teachers do not routinely consider that the bladder of a child might not hold very much. When a child is at a mall and asks the parent to find a bathroom, many parents presume the child is curious about the bathroom. When a child asks a teacher for permission to go to the bathroom, many teachers presume the child is trying to avoid class work. When a child gets up from the supper table to pee, many parents presume the child is trying to avoid finishing the supper. In all of these situations, the majority of children really do need to pee. How frequently they need to pee depends on what and how much they drink, and also on personality and behaviour.

In this chapter, I discuss how personality and behaviour play a role. In the next chapter, I will discuss how what they drink and how much they drink are also other important factors.

Some children are very attentive to their bladder signals, and they can tell me when they are full with remarkable consistency. In the office, these children pee similar volumes with great emptying and normal pee curves. These children are in the minority. About 10 or 20 per cent of the children that I see are attentive voiders and have what I refer to as an attentive bladder personality.

Some of these children are referred to me because they void frequently. They usually also wet the bed or get up several times to pee, but the real problem for the parents and the child is the frequent voiding. These children can void as often as every ten or fifteen minutes, and this pattern has a serious impact on the quality of family life. These parents cannot accomplish much on outings because they are always interrupting their activities to find a bathroom. These families do not do road trips. They do not travel to Disneyland. They stay pretty close to home.

There are more girls than boys who have an attentive bladder personality.

A remarkable number of these little girls come to my office wearing a dress. Pink is almost always their favourite colour. The dress is great for twirling, and many of the dresses have a princess theme.

When one of these girls turns up in my office, I describe her problem as "The Princess and the Pea Syndrome."

Most parents are familiar with this Hans Christian Andersen fairytale. A prince wants to marry a princess. The prince cannot figure out who is a real princess. One stormy night, a young woman drenched with rain seeks shelter in the prince's castle. She claims to be a princess, so the mother of the prince tests this claim by placing a pea in the bed the young woman will sleep in. The pea is placed beneath twenty mattresses and twenty feather beds. In the morning, the young woman remarks that she had a terrible sleep. She explains that something hard in the bed kept her up all night. The prince is thrilled. Finally, he has found his bride, because only a real princess would be able to feel a pea through so much bedding. The prince marries the young woman, and they live happily ever after.

This is a story about a person—a princess—who was much more attentive to the subtle pressure of a solitary pea under multiple mattresses than other people. In a similar fashion, the girls I see are much more attentive to the subtle pressure of poop on their bladder. The princess suffered a sleepless night, and the girls I see suffer multiple trips to the bathroom.

Parents who know this fairy tale instantly understand the analogy and relate how this fits "perfectly" with their daughter.

Most of these girls score high on the "perfectionist" or "meticulous" scale. Their rooms are very tidy and organized. They choose their clothes with care.

These girls are not prepared to risk dampness in the underwear, and if they ever did have a few drips in their underwear, they would need to change immediately. Just the thought of damp underwear is enough to bother these girls. In situations when there is no bathroom access, such as on car trips, they are likely to panic when they feel the first signal of a full bladder.

The majority of children are not this attentive; they are prepared to ignore the signals of a full bladder, and they do so for a variety of reasons that make good sense to them.

Most children would rather play than pee. Parents note that while engaged in very compelling play activities, these children employ a variety of common postures to postpone the trip to the bathroom. Common postures include fidgeting, toe tapping, squeezing the legs together, grabbing the groin area outside of the clothes, and for some boys, putting their hand in their pocket and squeezing the end of the penis. In my office, the most common early sign of a full bladder is when the child suddenly moves forward in the chair and sits on the edge. Eventually, these children cannot hold the pee any longer, and they race to the bathroom. Some children make it without wetting; others are damp, and some are soaked. As these children get older and more practiced, they learn to make it to the bathroom without major change-the-clothes wetting, but minor dampness can persist into adolescence.

Video games are especially compelling for some children. Many of these children will wet during the game and keep on playing in soaked clothes. I call this the "PlayStation piddle, the "Wii wee," or the "DS drip."

Establishing the volume for full in these children is not as easy as in the children who are attentive voiders, but over the course of the first visit and with regular reminders to tell me "sooner," I usually get a good estimate. Part of this exercise is to educate the child about the correct sense of fullness. Many times, this is the first time anyone has explained how their bladder works without criticizing their behaviour.

The next pages are the handouts on good bladder health that parents take away from my office.

Bobby
Good Bladder Health

Keep your bladder relaxed.

Pee more often, and pee to empty,
rather than always respond to the signal of full.

Pee at the common transition times, such as when you wake, before you leave the house to go to school or to play, when you are in the bathroom to wash your hands before a meal, before you sit down to watch television or to play a video game, and before bed.

Always respond to the signal of the need to pee. Don't hold.

Boys should sit to pee at home.
Always use great posture.
Sit in the middle of the toilet with the knees apart
and the feet flat on the ground or a footstool.
Smaller children need an over-the-toilet seat to achieve good posture.

Relax. Don't rush. Don't push.
Let the pee come out naturally.

At public urinals, pull your zipper or pants down
so the penis is not bent during voiding.

Betty
Good Bladder Health

Keep your bladder relaxed.

Pee more often, and pee to empty,
rather than always respond to the signal of full.

Pee at the common transition times, such as when you wake,
before you leave the house to go to school or to play, when you
are in the bathroom to wash your hands before a meal, before
you sit down to watch television or to play a video game, and
before bed.

Always respond to the signal of the need to pee. Don't hold.

Always use great posture.
Sit in the middle of the toilet with the knees apart
and the feet flat on the ground or a footstool.
Smaller children need an over-the-toilet seat to achieve good
posture.

Relax. Don't rush. Don't push.
Let the pee come out naturally.

Some children hold their pee with every void and every day. Others only hold when they are in special circumstances and access to a bathroom is restricted.

Children spend most of their waking day at school, and there are many obstacles to bathroom access in schools. Teachers commonly restrict access to a bathroom. Many teachers seem to believe that all children have the same size of bladder, and some of them must believe that the bladder of a child can hold as much as that of an adult.

Teachers commonly set limits on how often a child may void, on when a child may void, and on whether more than one child can attend the bathroom at the same time. Some teachers believe that children should always wait for scheduled breaks, such as recess or lunch. I often ask early elementary school–aged children to tell me what they like most about school. By far, the most common answer is "recess." Teachers who ask children to wait for recess must believe that the socializing that occurs at recess is less important to the young elementary school–aged child than the course syllabus. My own sense is that the socializing that happens at recess is every bit as important as the course syllabus.

Some teachers actually penalize children for using the bathroom; privileges are restricted, and rewards are removed. In a study I completed in 2006, I found that 5 per cent of teachers at schools in Southern Alberta penalized children for using the bathroom.

I was shocked to learn of the various punitive rules that teachers had set up to restrict access to the bathroom.

In a grade-three classroom, the children were "fined" every time they went to the bathroom. All the children were given play money at the start of each month. The money was used to purchase toys or books at the end of each month. Whenever the children did something good, such as completing an assignment on time, they received extra play money. Whenever the children did something bad, they lost some of their play money. The bad category included talking back to the teacher, not putting the chair up at the end of the day, failing to complete assignments, and requesting to go to the bathroom!

In a grade-five classroom, the students were required to practice the six Ps. The six Ps included the attributes of being polite, prompt, prepared, productive, persistent, and planet active. When a student did not adhere to these standards, the penalty was lack of access to the bathroom during class time for an entire week. My recommendation to that teacher was to add a seventh P, for pee..

In a grade-one classroom, the penalty for using the bathroom during class time was that the student was not allowed to go out for recess that day.

In a grade-three and grade-four split classroom, the teacher penalized one student by making the boy stay in at recess and do extra homework. This boy eventually dreaded school to the extent that he cried at home each morning before school, and his mother was concerned because he showed signs of depression. This mother started to homeschool her son in February of the school year.

In one grade-three classroom, if a child requested access to the bathroom, the teacher threatened to tell the parents or to write a note to the parents.

When teachers do allow access, they often set up elaborate rituals to use the bathroom, and they almost always request that the children ask permission. Children do not need to request permission to use a bathroom at home; why should they at school? Some children are shy and are reluctant to request permission to leave the class. Some are embarrassed to ask because they do not want their classmates to know they need to pee. Some are reluctant to make the journey alone from the classroom to the bathroom. In older schools, the bathroom might be on a different floor, through multiple sets of heavy doors, or even in a separate building, especially if portable classrooms are used. Some children are reluctant to use a school bathroom because the facilities are dirty or smelly. Witnessing one flooded toilet overflowing with poop that has plugged it is enough to chronically affect bathroom behaviour in lots of children. Older children may share the bathroom with younger children, and bullying can occur in bathrooms.

The rituals to access the bathroom often include an object that the child must place on his desk so that the teacher knows where the child has gone. One teacher with a sense of humour used a toilet plunger. A Winnie the Pooh stuffy is a fairly common object.

For the record, I believe children of all ages should be allowed to leave class to use the bathroom as often as required to respond to the signal of full. Any system that requires permission to leave should be simple and discreet. School bathrooms should be kept clean and monitored for bullying during the break times. Children should never be punished for the need to use the bathroom. I consider penalizing a child for peeing a form of child abuse.

Restricting access to a bathroom at school teaches children to ignore the signal. Should we be surprised when children continue to hold the pee at home as well?

Children need to be empowered to use the bathroom at school. For kindergarten and early elementary–aged children, I recommend that parents take their child to school on the first day of each new school year. The parent should identify the bathroom for that classroom. I ask the parents to walk with their child from the classroom to the bathroom so that the child knows the way. The parent should go into the bathroom and give the bathroom the mommy or daddy "seal of approval." The parent should explain the practical aspects of how to choose a clean toilet, how to clean a toilet seat, how to lock the cubicle door, and how to wash the hands afterwards. On that first day, the parent should specifically talk with the teacher in front of her child and state that her child should be excused to pee as often as necessary. I write notes for hundreds of parents every year to make this crystal clear to the teachers. If the child hears the parent state that he can pee whenever he needs to and if the teacher agrees to this in front of the child, this empowers the child to pay attention to the signal of a full bladder. If the teacher does not agree, ask your doctor for a note. If the teacher still doesn't agree, ask your doctor to write a letter to the principal. I've only had to do that a very few times; most teachers are happy to help once the situation is explained.

The following is an example of the note I send to the teacher.

November 3, 2010

Bobby

Dear Grade-Three Elbow Valley Schoolteacher,

Please allow Bobby to leave class as necessary to pee. He should not be requested to wait for scheduled breaks. He should not be obliged to wait if another child is in the bathroom. He should be allowed to leave class about five or ten minutes before the end of the school day so he is not in a rush to pee before he gets on the school bus.

Please allow Bobby to have a water bottle at his desk and to drink throughout the school day.

Thank you for helping.

Lane Robson, MD

Some parents encourage their child to hold the pee. They don't take the time to find a bathroom in the mall, or they don't stop the car on road trips. Parents are often very busy and sometimes too busy to allow their child access to a bathroom.

Some parents encourage their child to hold the pee because they believe or were told that their child could "stretch" the bladder and increase the size by holding. *Ouch!* This is so wrong.

We need to teach our children to pay attention to the body's signals, not ignore them. When we are tired, we should rest. When we are thirsty, we should drink. When we are cold, we should put on more clothes. When we need to pee, we should pee.

Holding the pee is not only wrong generally, but at the extreme end of the spectrum of this behaviour, there is the possibility of serious, long-term damage to the bladder.

I can tell how often a child holds his pee by assessing the thickness of the bladder wall. The bladder is a muscle, and as with all muscles, the thickness increases with exercise. For bladder walls, big is not better; thin is in.

Some children learn to really control their sphincter muscle at the bottom of the bladder, and they can hold their bladder under terrific pressure without even a drop escaping. At least once a month, I will assess a child, more often a boy, who tells me he can "really hold it." These children can often describe mental and physical strategies that allow them to stay bone-dry with a bladder that is under great pressure. These children worry me. I would rather these children wet and let off the pressure. If this practice continues into adolescence, some of these children might permanently lose bladder function.

One adolescent who told me, "I can really hold it," went on to clarify that "I must tell myself to hold it in," and this takes "every last bit of my concentration." He told me that if he thought of anything else, he would soak himself.

This boy explained an extreme case of a common situation.

Have you ever been in a meeting or a social situation when you really had to pee, but you could not conveniently leave to use the bathroom? Most people have experienced this, and if you have, you also know that your mind was not very attentive to that meeting or to that social situation. Your mind was precisely focused on keeping the pee in your bladder.

Now, think of an elementary classroom and consider the teachers who restrict access to the bathroom so that the children do not miss any teaching. Do you think those children who are holding their pee are really learning anything?

When parents see their child posturing, they commonly suggest, "Time to go to the bathroom."

The children often respond, "I don't have to," notwithstanding the obvious holding postures.

In some homes, this deteriorates into a confrontation.

When parents find their child playing in wet clothes, they commonly ask, "Didn't you know you had to go?"

The child often responds, "I didn't know," or "I didn't feel it until it was too late."

33

These situations lead some parents to wonder whether the nerves are hooked up properly. The nerves are fine in 99.9 per cent of these children.

First of all, I tell parents that the nerves are okay, and then I tell them that the child is not lying. I discuss several possible explanations for this behaviour.

The first explanation is that the bladder signals have become "background noise." Most everyone understands this concept. Our brain filters out lots of background noise. The noise is there, and the brain registers the noise, but since we don't prefer to be distracted by the noise, we allow our brains to help us out and suppress the incoming information. I believe the same thing happens to children with bladder signals. The signals have become "background noise." The nerve is fine, and the signals are there, but the boy instructed his brain a long time ago not to bother him with these signals. The child is not lying; he really doesn't recollect the signals. When I teach the children in the clinic to tell me "sooner," I am helping them to get back in touch with these signals.

Another explanation is that the child might have a "processing" problem. Processing problems are common in children with a variety of learning problems, including children with ADHD/ADD.

Daytime wetting, bedwetting, constipation, and soiling are more common in children with these problems. In 1997, I published a study on the frequency of daytime wetting, nighttime wetting, and soiling in children with ADHD. Our study was the first large controlled study of this relationship.

Children with a processing problem do not multitask well. They handle one thing at a time okay, but they have problems as soon as they are expected to process something different at the same time. A signal to pee is something different for these children.

When I mention problems with multitasking to the mothers, a surprising number laugh and remark, "Like his father."

Many parents presume that their child thinks like an adult. They presume that the child understands that daytime wetting is not acceptable. Piaget, a famous child psychologist, clarified the stages in the intellectual and psychological development of a child. He differentiated Early Childhood as a distinct stage that precedes Middle Childhood, and he reported that the transition to Middle Childhood generally occurs between the ages of six and eight years. Piaget points out that during Early Childhood, a child is "ego-centric," and he only views the world from his own perspective. He does not see himself as others do, not even his peers. Until he makes the transition to Middle Childhood, he will not even remotely be thinking like an adult. Until he makes this transition, he might not personally have any reason to work on dryness. Until he makes this transition, he cannot "see" himself with holding postures or playing in wet clothes.

Some children just wet. They make no pretence of running to the bathroom. My sense is that some of these children have acknowledged that they cannot make it to the bathroom on time, so they don't bother.

I recollect one six-year-old girl who had day and night wetting. She soaked her clothes several times every day. I had followed her for about six months without any real progress; she had not improved her bowel health. At one visit, while I was talking with Mom in my office and she was in the play area, my assistant overheard her talking to another little girl who was waiting for her appointment. The other little girl was doing the pee dance, and the six-year-old told her, "Just pee your pants. I do it all the time."

This is especially common in children with an autism spectrum disorder. Many of these children do not do anything that doesn't make sense to them. Their view of the world is different. Their sense of logic is different. They know they won't make it on time if they run, so why bother? Why not just wet and carry on with what they really want to do?

Now we have learned that how often a child pees and whether and how much they wet depends on personality, age, bathroom access, and whether the child has certain learning and behavioural problems.

What is common in all of these situations is the poop wall.

Children who routinely run to the bathroom are up against the poop wall.

Some parents believe that their child would ignore the signals even if they were not up against the poop wall. Most of these parents are implying that their child is wilfully stubborn. There might be a few wilfully stubborn children with bladder-friendly bowel health and a normal bladder capacity, but I've never encountered one in my office.

To my mind, the question of why a child with a wilful or a stubborn personality wets by day is a "Which came first, the chicken or the egg?" kind of argument. If children had a bladder that could hold more, and if they had good access to a bathroom, I believe that even a wilful or stubborn child would learn to pay attention to the signals, would be able to walk to the bathroom, and would always be dry. I think the poop wall is what set them up in the first place. I think the poop wall is the "egg" from which the tendency to ignore the signals is "hatched."

Some parents suggest that their child could make a choice to go more often. These parents are implying that these children can change their personality, and I do not believe this is a simple choice for these children.

If we view playing as an "addiction," then these children really do not have any "choice." Dr. Gabor Mate is a physician who has worked with Vancouver homeless and addicts for many years. In his book, *In the Realm of Hungry Ghosts*, Mate explains that addiction is not a choice. Addicts cannot just stop whatever they are addicted to. Individuals can be addicted to a wide range of behaviours, including video games. An addiction could be defined as any chronic behaviour that stimulates neurotransmitter chemicals in the brain and consistently results in a powerful sense of satisfaction. When the neurotransmitters in the brain consistently reward the chronic behaviour, this becomes an ingrained pattern. If these neurotransmitters are operative in children who play video games, or even in children who genuinely enjoy any compelling and repetitive play activity, then I can well imagine that these children do not really have a "choice."

Helping a child to gain daytime bladder control is very satisfying. As the bowel health improves, these children stop running to the bathroom and the dampness and the wetting disappear. They learn that they can hold more if they need to without risking the mad dash. They learn that they can have a big glass of water or juice without worrying about where the nearest bathroom is. They know their bladder can hold more. They tell me that the pee takes longer to come out. The parents tell me that they don't need to stop as often on road trips or get up to pee during the most exciting part of the movie. For those children who never paid attention to the signals at all and who just wet, they start to pay attention and actually go to the bathroom. When these children start to pay attention to their bladders for the first time, the mothers are ecstatic. I call this first contact, and this is almost as satisfying for me as when they are dry at night.

Why Don't All Children with Constipation Wet the Bed?

I think the timing of constipation and the severity of the constipation are important factors.

A small percentage of the children who are referred to me are wet by day but dry at night. These children have urgency and daytime wetting, and the poop wall is the major factor in their daytime symptoms. They are dry at night, and this is either because they wake up to pee or because their bladder can hold enough urine for the amount of pee that is produced. The bowel health is often worse in these children than in those who present with bedwetting as well. The diameter of the rectum is wider and soiling is more common. The constipation in these children almost always starts during the first two years of life and usually within the first year. My theory is that these children have had so much poop in their pelvis from early infancy that the poop has literally pushed the bladder out of the pelvis, and the bladder has learned to hold more urine because of this out-of-the-pelvis location. The pelvic ultrasound of these children often shows the top of the bladder almost up to the belly button, with the largest volume outside of the pelvis, and a narrow tube of bladder that runs out of the pelvis just under the abdominal wall. The pictures make the bladder look like a big mushroom with the stalk in the pelvis. I call this the mushroom sign. These children might be dry at night, but their bladder capacities are still not normal, only better than those who do wet at night.

Below on the left is an ultrasound image from a ten and three quarters-year-old boy who had urgency and daytime wetting but was dry at night. He also had a longstanding history of constipation and soiling. He pooped his pants almost every day. The mother was more worried about the soiling than the daytime wetting, which is appropriate. The image shows the mushroom sign. This is a lateral view. At the top of the image is the skin surface of the abdomen. The pee and poop come out on the right side of this image. The belly button is to the left of this image. Note the narrow bladder tube squished against the abdominal wall by the poop below. Once the bladder is no longer constrained by the poop and the pelvic bones, the bladder expands into the abdominal cavity.

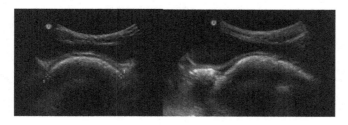

The image on the right is the front view in the same child. This bladder really has a frown ☹. There is so much poop in the rectum at the bottom of the pelvis that the bladder is squished right against the tummy wall. The distance between the two points marked by the number 1 is 67 millimetres (almost three inches)! This boy was really tired of his constipation and soiling. What boy in grade five wants to poop his pants? He followed my recommendations to the letter, and at the two-month follow-up, he was pooping twice a day and the soiling was gone. His mom told me, "It's a miracle." After a decade of poop problems, I'm sure it must feel like that to the mom.

I believe that the children who wet the bed develop their bowel problems when they are a little older, by which time the size of the pelvis is big enough that the bladder does not "escape" outside the pelvis and the bladder capacity is more significantly compromised. These children often develop their bowel problems around toilet training. This is almost certainly the case in the 25 per cent of children who develop their bedwetting after a period of initial dryness.

Where Did All That Pee Come From?

Our kidneys make the pee. There is one kidney on each side, under the ribs at the back of the abdomen. A ureter tube carries urine from the kidney to the bladder. The tube has muscle and actually squirts the urine into the bladder.

When I do an ultrasound and the urine is being produced quickly, I show the children the urine squirts as they come into the bladder. Modern ultrasound technology can visualize flow, and I can choose any colour for the flow. I have my ultrasound set up to show the urine a bright orange. The squirts look like flames coming into the bladder, and the children enjoy these images. The squirts come in at an angle towards the middle, and when a squirt comes in from each side at the same time, the squirts cross each other. "Like duelling light sabres," I explain, and this almost always brings a smile from the boys.

Kidneys are filter organs. Everything we eat or drink is digested in the stomach and intestine, absorbed into the blood, and filtered through the kidneys. The kidneys are obliged to process what we eat or drink promptly. A healthy kidney does not get behind on the filter work. This means that what you eat at dinner is filtered overnight.

The kidneys are in charge of regulating the salt and water balance in the body. When there is too much salt or water, the kidney dumps the excess. When there is too little, the kidney holds on to the salt and water.

Making sure we have the right amount of salt and water in the body is a very important job. Without efficient kidneys, we could swing from too much fluid (heart failure) to too little fluid (shock), and this can happen when our kidneys fail.

Our bodies constantly use and lose water.

We need water for each new cell, and children grow every minute of every hour for twenty-four hours each and every day. Children grow while they are awake and while they are asleep. Each new cell is about two-thirds water.

We lose water through our skin and our lungs and in our urine and poop. In children with bedwetting, there is not much water lost in their poop. Hard and pasty poop does not have much water content.

Overnight, children perspire into their cozy sheets, and some wake up really wet, especially on hot summer nights. If the child did not sweat, the body temperature would go up in an unhealthy fashion. Therefore, the body does not allow the skin to stop sweating.

Every breath we exhale contains water (think of breathing on a window when the temperature is cold). The lungs need to be bathed in water vapour to stay healthy. Therefore, the body does not allow the lungs to dry out.

The kidneys clean the blood and are obliged to be prompt about cleaning out the waste products. The waste is excreted as a liquid, and so the kidney needs water to do its job.

In an earlier chapter, I mentioned that five-year-old children sleep for eleven hours a night, or almost half the entire day. Even by adolescence, the child is still sleeping at least a third of the entire day. The need for water does not stop overnight. The child still grows, the lungs still breathe, the skin still sweats, and the kidneys still make pee.

The child sleeps, but the kidneys never sleep.

Children don't usually drink overnight, and many bedwetting children are fluid restricted by their parents in the evening. This means that when a child wakes up, he is already behind on his fluid needs for the day.

If a child has supper, but afterwards the parents restrict the fluid intake and the child goes to bed thirsty and then doesn't drink overnight, where does this leave the body? The body still needs water—water to grow, water to keep the lungs moist, water to perspire, and water to make pee.

What is the body to do in this situation?

Well, the body does not just wait for morning. The body goes to the only place where water is available. The body goes to the bowel and sucks out as much water as possible to meet the need. The water content from the food at supper and with the evening snack is scavenged for water. Water is pulled out from the large intestine or colon, the last 20 per cent of the bowel. The poop at the bottom becomes hard. The poop higher up becomes pasty.

You might think that children would invariably wake up the next morning thirsty in this situation, but this is not the case. Most children who wet the bed are not thirsty in the morning. These children often come home from school thirsty and are almost always thirsty at bedtime but not at breakfast.

They manage to suck out enough water overnight from the bowel to prevent thirst the next morning.

There is a thirst centre in our brain that tells us when we need to drink water. This centre tells a child to drink when the amount of fluid outside the cells falls by about 5 per cent, or when the concentration of sodium and other chemicals in the blood goes up. The latter is the reason why eating salty foods leads to thirst. When the amount of fluid outside the cells falls by about 10 per cent, children start to feel dizzy when they get up quickly from lying or sitting, and they can develop headaches. The blood pressure in these children is borderline low. The blood pressure falls below normal and shock sets in when the amount of fluid outside the cells falls by 15 per cent.

Almost all children with bedwetting are thirsty at bedtime and therefore potentially at least 5 per cent behind on their fluids. I sometimes see children with dizziness as a result of getting up from lying or standing, and this symptom suggests these children are about 10 per cent behind. Almost shocking (pun intended)!

Now, let's consider a situation when the bladder has never held enough since infancy. Let's consider someone like Bobby, who has likely always had a bladder that has not held enough and who also has a personality that is prepared to ignore bladder signals during play. When he was a toddler, his parents were likely always on his case to pee more often, especially when they saw him posturing. He likely wet his pants a lot, and perhaps his parents periodically scolded him for wetting. At day care or preschool, the caregivers or teachers might have been critical when he had an accident. Perhaps someone shamed him. His running and wetting continued through kindergarten and grade one, and likely during these years, he was exposed to even more adults who were critical of his daytime wetting. No one was happy on the days when his mother had to come to the school with a change of clothes. By the time Bobby reached grade one, he knew several things for sure: wetting his pants was bad; he never wanted to miss out on playtime at snack and recess; and he never seemed to make it to the bathroom on time.

What was Bobby to do?

At some point along the way, Bobby realized that after he drank anything, he needed to pee. He also realized that when he drank water, juice, or pop that he had to pee sooner and more often than if he drank milk. So, Bobby stopped drinking at breakfast and during the school day, and when he did drink, he chose milk. Bobby did this to minimize his need to go to the bathroom, to minimize his risk of wetting, and to maximize his time playing with his friends.

There are various patterns that emerge.

A very common pattern is for the child to choose milk at breakfast and lunch and then to start drinking juice or water once he gets home. For these children, this means that they go to bed thirsty (5 per cent behind), the body scavenges enough water from the bowel overnight to prevent thirst at breakfast, and then they don't drink anything but milk until they get back home at about 3:30 p.m. If they go to bed thirsty at 8:30 p.m. and only start to satisfy their thirst the next day at 3:30 p.m., they go nineteen hours in a thirsty or almost-thirsty state. Then in the five hours from arriving home until bedtime, they drink the majority of their total daily fluids as water or juice. This pattern guarantees a lot of pee production overnight and also guarantees a high rate of pee production in the first few hours after falling asleep. I call this the "evening surge" in pee production. These children are always wet; they often wet within two or three hours of falling asleep and then again later. They might also soak through their pull-ups into the bedsheets.

Some children only drink milk the entire day, and they drink a lot of milk. They have a cup at breakfast and more on their cereal, a cup at lunch, a cup when they get home, two cups with supper, and their bedtime snack is often cereal with milk. These children are always thirsty; they satisfy this thirst only with milk; and they are often chronically dehydrated. Their poops are very hard, and the amount their bladder can hold is at the lower end of the spectrum. They are always wet, but they do not usually soak through their pull-up into the bedsheets. Some of them wake up at night thirsty, or they are thirsty when they wake up. Some of these children wake up to drink, but not to pee!

Some children drink absolutely nothing at breakfast, and their only drink during the day is a brief stop at the water fountain after gym at school. Their parents send them with water bottles or juice boxes, but they come back full. Their entire daily fluid intake is in the five hours from arriving home until bedtime. They are always wet, and depending on how much they drink, they might or might not soak through the pull-up into the bedsheets.

Some children drink milk at breakfast, milk at lunch, and then milk after school, but nothing from then until bedtime. These children are chronically dehydrated, have very hard poop, and their bladder does not hold very much, but they have dry nights, because they are so disciplined about their fluid intake in the late afternoon and evening. Their parents are usually happy about the dry nights, but they have no idea about how poorly hydrated their child is. These children often have dizziness when getting up quickly and headaches.

Older children who still wet the bed often report, "I know I can be dry if I stay up late." Lots of older elementary-aged children eventually figure this out, and when the wetting persists into adolescence, this is the most common strategy for dryness when the children attend a sleepover. They don't drink much in the evening, and they stay up much later than usual; when they make sure to pee just before they fall asleep, they have emptied out the "evening surge." The amount of pee that is produced for the remainder of the night fits in the bladder, and they wake up dry.

I remember a fourteen-year-old boy who wet the bed almost every night. He was a husky adolescent, and he played football for one of the junior teams in the city. He didn't want to be in my office; he certainly didn't want to talk about his bedwetting, and he made his feelings very clear within moments of his arrival. He was a very angry and aggressive boy who was regularly rude to both his mother and me. He was too big to wear a pull-up, and he soaked the sheets every day. His mother was the person who did the laundry. I reviewed my recommendations to cure his bedwetting, but he would have nothing to do with my suggestions.

"Don't you want to be dry?" I asked.

"I can be dry anytime I want," he replied. "I go on lots of sleepovers, and I'm always dry. All I need to do is not drink much, stay up real late, and always pee before I go to bed."

This boy had enough control over his bedwetting to satisfy himself but not enough to satisfy his mother. Bedwetting that persists into adolescence can become an emotionally supercharged issue. Some adolescents take their frustrations out on their parents, most commonly on the mother. When an adolescent is this rude and verbally abusive to his mother in a public setting, I can only cringe at the thought of how these feelings might play out in the home.

Managing hydration at school can be a real challenge. Many teachers do not allow a water bottle at the desk, and they generally only allow children to have water in the bottle. Some children will not drink water, but they will drink juice, flavoured water, or iced tea. These teachers will allow the child to have a water bottle in their pack that hangs by the entrance to the classroom, and they only allow the children to access the pack at break times or when the child requests permission. These teachers restrict access to the water bottle in the same fashion as teachers restrict access to the bathroom. They restrict water bottles for a variety of well-meaning (from their perspective) reasons. They don't want the children to spill water on books and papers. They don't want children to play with the water. They don't want children to drink so much that they need to leave the classroom to pee.

Again, for the record, I believe children should be allowed water bottles at their desk, they should be allowed to have whatever healthy fluid suits their fancy, and they should be able to leave class as necessary to pee.

Most children cannot tell me that they purposefully do not drink much on school days. They don't realize how or when they made this intuitive decision, but many can and do tell me that they pee different on weekends. They usually pee more often on weekends, and when I ask them why, they reply, "Because I drink more." Then I ask them to comment on why they pee less at school, and they realize and respond, "Because I drink less."

Back to Bobby

Bobby's mother brought him to my office.

The children are usually in the play area before their appointment time, and after I finish the paperwork on the last patient, I walk out and say hello to the next child. My usual pattern is to walk into the play area and to ask if there is a Bobby around. I make eye contact and speak directly to the child. I purposefully don't speak to the parent; I want the child to know that he is the centre of attention for me. How the child responds will be my first clue about the personality and behaviour of the child. Most are very pleased to be the centre of attention, but not all. Some will smile and continue playing; some will stand up politely; and others will totally ignore me.

I carry on.

"My name is Dr. Robson. How are you today, Bobby?"

For a few minutes, I talk with Bobby about his Calgary Flames jersey. For other children, I might talk about the toys, their hairstyle, the weather, or whatever seems appropriate for the child.

Then I ask Bobby to come with me and to bring his mother with him. From then on, my focus is mostly on the child and how he reacts during the next two hours.

I take Bobby and his mother back to the ultrasound room.

"The first thing we do is take a picture of your tummy. It doesn't hurt, and it's really fun."

If the child looks apprehensive, I reassure him that his mother can stay right with him.

Once the child is lying on the ultrasound table, I explain what I am going to do.

Before I put the ultrasound transducer on his lower tummy, I ask Bobby whether he needs to pee.

Bobby hesitates and replies, "Sort of."

So I help him clarify this for me.

"If you were at home and not doing anything special and the bathroom was real close, would you be going pee if you felt this way?"

Bobby replies, "Yes."

"Okay," I respond. "How about if you were at school? Would you be asking the teacher to leave the class if you felt this way?"

Bobby replies, "No. She doesn't let us leave the class."

Then I ask, "How about if you were at a mall with your mother and you felt this way. Would you ask your mom to find a bathroom?"

Bobby replies, "Yes, but my dad wouldn't. He'd tell me to hold it till we got home."

By now, I have lots of information about Bobby, his school, and his home. Bobby would choose to be more attentive if he could, but there are access issues at his school and Dad is not helping him to be attentive.

Now I put the ultrasound transducer on his abdomen, and I take the first look.

I have used an ultrasound to assess the bladder for about twenty years, but until I opened my bedwetting clinic in Calgary, I never did the ultrasound examination myself. There was always a technician or nurse who did the ultrasound. Deciding to do the ultrasound myself was likely the most important learning decision I've ever made. This book would not have been written had I not made that decision. I would never have understood the real story about bedwetting had I not made that decision. I have learned more about bedwetting in the last five years than I learned in all of the prior twenty-five years. Every doctor who treats bedwetting should do his or her own ultrasounds, but very few do.

I purchased a very expensive ultrasound so that I would have the best image quality. I read papers on ultrasound technology and technique, and I visited X-ray departments in different countries. I asked the X-ray doctors who did the ultrasounds a lot of questions. What I learned asking questions was that many of the ultrasound doctors didn't know much about the bladder. The bladder was sort of an uncharted territory.

When I started, I felt like an explorer going where no paediatric bladder doctor had ever gone before. Then I practiced, and practice makes perfect.

I always explain to the child what I will do.

"Bobby, I'm going to take a picture of your bladder. I'll put some jelly on your tummy to help take the picture. The jelly will feel a little cold. Are you ready for a jelly belly?"

When I started out, I only looked at the bladder. I'm a urine doctor, so I looked at the urine. Now, my first look is at the rectum. In children with bedwetting, the diameter of the rectum is almost always wider than normal, and commonly greater than the 30 millimetres that implies a diagnosis of constipation. A normal number would be 20 to 25 millimetres. Bobby's rectum measured 42 millimetres. Most of the children I see have a diameter in the thirties (more than an inch), about a quarter in the forties (almost two inches), and perhaps 10 per cent in the 50s and 60s (greater than two inches). The largest diameter I ever saw was in the 80s (more than three inches). Ouch!

Next, I assess what the poop looks like. Poop that is bright white on the ultrasound is very hard poop. The sound waves are bounced right back, like off bone. Soft poop allows some sound waves to travel through, and the colour is variable shades of grey. The urine in the bladder allows all the sound waves to travel through and is black. The shapes of the poop vary from logs to balls. Lateral images show various kinds of poop lined up ready to come out. Generally, the poop in the children who wet the bed is hard at the very bottom and pasty above that. Bobby's poop was more white than grey, and I could see poop balls and logs.

As I pressed the transducer to get different images, I noticed Bobby move his legs a bit.

"Are you okay?" I asked.

"I have to go now," he replies.

He is full. The mild pressure of the transducer is enough to give him urgency.

"Okay," I reply and take a last quick look before I let him go to pee. I have learned to judge just how much time I have before they wet on the table. I'm not perfect though. Several times a year, I will be looking at a full bladder that disappears as the child empties on my ultrasound table. Most parents do not bring a change of clothes. I have a washer and dryer in the office, and these children wear a gown until their clothes are dry.

I look at the bladder shape, check to see if the ureter tubes are visible, and assess the regularity and thickness of the bladder wall.

Bobby's bladder is squished in the middle by the pasty poop in his rectum. I do not see the ureter tubes. His bladder wall has a consistent calibre but looks a bit thick.

I clean the gel off Bobby's abdomen and ask him to follow me to the pee room.

As we walk, I ask Bobby if he usually sits or stands to pee.

"I stand," he responds.

"Okay, here is where I want you to stand. I want you to pull your pants and underwear down to your knees, hold your penis, and direct all the pee into the centre of the toilet. Mom will supervise. After you pee, I want you

47

to come right back to the ultrasound room. Don't wash your hands. I want to find out how well you emptied right away."

I leave the room and wait. Some boys are back out in fewer than thirty seconds, and others take several minutes. Bobby is out very quickly.

> Okay, Bobby, hippity hop,
> Up to the top,
> Back on the table,
> Fast as you're able.

He climbs back up on the ultrasound table, and I check out the empty bladder. The definition of good emptying, according to the International Children's Continence Society (ICCS), is that there should be less than one teaspoon (5 millilitres) left in the bladder. I know that a healthy bladder that is full but relaxed can empty and leave only a few drops. For me, the presence of even a teaspoon means that the bladder is actually overfull. Bobby has 9.5 millilitres (almost two teaspoons) of urine remaining in his bladder. His bladder is definitely overfull.

With the first void at the first visit, the after-they-pee image usually shows more than a teaspoon of urine, and depending how overfull the bladder is, I sometimes see an ounce (30 millilitres) or more. Some children have had a lot to drink prior to arriving at the office, and they are ready to burst with the first void. In these children, I don't take the before-they-pee ultrasound images. If they are jumping up and down or if they tell me they can't hold it, I quickly explain about posture and let them pee in the Uroflow toilet.

Bobby's bladder wall looked a bit thick, and the measurement was 4.1 millimetres. The definition of a thick bladder is more than 5 millimetres when the bladder is empty and has less than 5 ml of urine. I consider 2.5 to 3 millimetres average and healthy. Bobby's bladder wall is a bit thicker than average, and this implies that he holds his pee, which fits well with the story.

The rectum under the empty bladder is still wide, but at this lower level under the empty bladder and just above the anus, the rectum is now 26 millimetres and the stool is very hard. A normal number at this level would be 15 to 18 millimetres.

I wipe off the jelly and ask Bobby to wash his hands while I retrieve the Uroflow result. I always try to guess what the volume will be and what the curve will look like. This is a game I play with myself, and I am getting very good at it. This is part of the reason I decided to write this book. I figured that if I could predict what I would see, based on the story and the ultrasound, I must know what I'm doing.

Bobby is eight and a half years old. The bladder of a boy who is dry at night should hold an average of 310 millilitres (10 ounces). Bobby's bladder was overfull, and he peed only 125 millilitres.

A normal Uroflow curve is a bell shape. Once the bladder is past full, the shape first turns into a tower and then becomes flatter and broader. Bobby had a tower-shaped curve, which together with his fidgeting legs on the ultrasound table and the 9.5 millilitres of urine that remained in the bladder after he peed, confirms that his bladder was overfull. He managed with a conscious effort to hold in his pee. He can hold this much by day, but at night, he will empty when his bladder contains less urine. I want to find out how much less.

"Bobby, thanks for coming in with a full bladder and for cooperating so well with the ultrasound. I need you to drink some more water for me, and next time, I want you to tell me when you need to pee as soon as you feel full."

Bobby cooperates, and over the next two hours, he pees two more times. He is a good listener and wants to please, and he does pee sooner the next two times. The second time he peed 110 millilitres, left 4.5 millilitres in the bladder, and had a nearly normal bell-shaped curve.

"Even sooner next time," I asked Bobby, and the third time, he peed 95 millilitres, left only 2 millilitres in the bladder, and the curve was a bell shape.

His last pee is the best estimate of his relaxed bladder capacity, and this is the best estimate of how much his bladder can hold at night. With a bladder that only holds about three ounces, he likely empties his bladder multiple times overnight. Pull-ups for boys his age are very absorbent. A GoodNite™ or an UnderJam™ for a boy his size will hold more than eight to twelve ounces before overflowing. Based on this, he likely wets three or four times on the nights he has a heavy pull-up, and one more time on the nights he soaks through.

The week before I wrote this book, I made an inadvertent joke in the office. The child put his hand up to let me know that he needed to pee again, and I said, "Okay, let's go to the ultrasound room and take a leak."

Of course, I meant to say peek—pee, peek, and leak. Even the mom laughed.

In between the Uroflow and ultrasound tests, I ask a lot of questions, mostly of Bobby.

With Bobby, I clarify that he only pees once at school over lunch and that the teacher does restrict access to the bathroom. The rule is that children are only allowed to pee at scheduled breaks and if they need to leave class, it needs to be an "emergency." Bobby never takes time to pee at morning snack because he always sits with his best friend, and they always trade or show off their hockey cards. He does pee before he goes out for lunch recess because he has learned that the teachers lock the doors once all the children are outside, and in grade one, he would sometimes wet his pants during recess. He has chocolate milk at lunch, and by the end of the day he would like to pee, but there is a lot of pressure to go immediately from the classroom to the school bus. The teachers want the children out of their class quickly; school policy is that children should not be wandering the halls, and the school bus driver wants to leave promptly. There is a lineup of buses and schedules to meet. Usually, the last time Bobby has peed is three hours earlier, after lunch. The kidney has now processed lunch, and his bladder is pretty full. He is rushed onto the bus, and for the last half of the ride, he is usually pretty fidgety as he tries to hold in his pee. There is one section that is bumpy, and he often wets along this stretch. By the time he gets home, he is often bursting.

Hmmm. The school bus ride home would likely be a great place and time to screen children for bladder and bowel problems.

I also clarify that Bobby only poops on about half the days and that he can remember a time when he went almost a week without pooping.

"Bobby," his mom gasps, "you didn't!"

Bobby reports that he usually pushes to poop and that the poop is sometimes hard to get out and sometimes not.

On the pre-visit questionnaire, his mother wrote down that Bobby pooped every day.

Bobby relates that he drinks at least three four-ounce cups of water from the water cooler between getting home and supper. He acknowledges that he is thirsty on most at-home nights and that he drinks from the tap when he brushes his teeth.

He isn't thirsty at bedtime on hockey nights because the coach's assistant literally squirts water into the mouth of each boy every time the line changes. Mom reports that Bobby often comes home from hockey practices and games with his clothes soaked with pee. Bobby doesn't remember feeling full during hockey. Mothers are often puzzled that their child doesn't use the bathroom at the rink. Elementary school-aged boys do not want to miss a single second of the action. What if they left the bench and there was a line change and they missed out on some ice time? Or what if they weren't there when someone scored a goal?

After all the questions have been asked and I have a good sense of the size of Bobby's bladder, I have two more things to accomplish before we talk about treatment. I need to check his urine, and I need to do a complete physical exam. The urine test and the physical exam are important, but nothing is more important than taking a good history. A teacher in medical school taught me that if I take a good enough history, I will know what I will find on the examination.

I check Bobby's urine and find that the first urine he peed was very dark and concentrated. Whatever time of the day a child arrives for the first visit, the first pee is usually very dark and concentrated and the specific gravity test is high. The specific gravity test measures the concentration of chemicals in the urine, and the result can vary from 1.001 to 1.035. Dark urine and a high specific gravity means there is less water in the body and that the body is on the dry side, so the kidney is holding on to water. Pale urine and a low specific gravity means there is more water in the body and the body has more than enough water for current needs, so the kidney can pee out more water. Bobby's result was 1.033. This means that his body is making urine but very concentrated urine. His kidneys are trying to work with as little water as possible. Children who wet the bed are almost always behind on their fluids during the day.

I pointed this out to Bobby and his mother. I showed them the dark yellow urine from the first pee, and the lighter and finally pale urine with the next two pees.

Bobby offered, "Yeah, my urine never looks white like that."

I check for the presence of white blood cells or bacteria in the urine. White blood cells and bacteria suggest infection. Bobby's urine does not have signs of infection.

I check for the presence of red blood cells in the urine. Red blood cells might suggest a structural problem, such as a blockage in his urethra. Bobby's urine does not have red blood cells, and I already knew that he did not have a blockage in the urethra because his pee curve did not have an obstructive pattern.

Finally, I check the urine for sugar, because diabetes mellitus is a rare cause of bedwetting. Bobby's story does not suggest diabetes, but I always check because a surprising number of parents ask about this, and I like to be able to tell them there is no sugar in the urine.

I always do a complete exam. The ICCS does not recommend a complete exam for a child with bedwetting, but I disagree. A good general exam takes fewer than ten minutes, and while I might not find any physical cause to explain the bedwetting, I sometimes learn a lot about the child.

I start off with the blood pressure, and if the BP is borderline low, I think back to the hydration history and wonder if I need to ask more questions. I feel his palms and determine if he is cool or moist, sure signs of anxiety, and I'm often surprised at how calm the child has presented himself compared to his palms.

I do a good neurological exam of the lower extremities, since a neurogenic bladder is a rare cause of bedwetting, and this helps to reassure both the parent and me that a neurological cause is not present. When the time comes for a parent to ask if the nerves are okay, I want to be able to say that the exam did not suggest a nerve problem.

I feel the abdomen, and I am never surprised to feel the solid lump of poop emerging from the pelvis on the left and extending up towards the ribs on this side. Sometimes I feel a huge mass of poop in the middle of the lower abdomen.

A genitalia exam is often necessary. If I decide the exam is necessary, I always ask for the permission of the mother and then also of the child. Without permission, I will not perform the exam. When the child refuses permission, I respect this decision. Sometimes the parent tries to force the child to comply, but I do not allow this. Occasionally, the refusal to allow a genital exam is a clue to a past history of sexual abuse.

I started my career as a paediatric nephrologist (specialist in kidney problems in children), but as I learned more and more about the impact of bowel health on bladder function, there are some days when I think I am now more of a paediatric gastroenterologist (specialist in bowel problems in children). Most days, I listen and talk about behaviour enough to feel like a psychologist. Recently, a mother made a comment that underscored just how far I have evolved from my general paediatric and nephrology beginnings. The mother advised that her elementary-aged daughter had irritation in the genital area. Her urine had evidence of infection, and I advised the mom that I should check the genitalia. Her daughter looked concerned at this suggestion, so her mom reassured her with the comment, "It's okay, honey; he's a real doctor."

In uncircumcised boys, I always check that the foreskin retracts, and in a circumcised boy, I check what the pee hole looks like. The Uroflow curve in an uncircumcised boy with a foreskin that doesn't retract might look obstructive, so I need to know this. The pee hole in boys who are circumcised is commonly small. This is called meatal stenosis, and this is almost always due to the pee hole closing up due to the irritation and inflammation immediately after the circumcision. A small pee hole also causes an obstructive Uroflow curve, which is important to know. If there is a web across the pee hole of a circumcised boy, this is the explanation for a stream that is deflected up. Bedwetting has nothing to do with whether the foreskin retracts or not and nothing to do with the size of the pee hole in a circumcised boy.

For the record, I don't recommend routine circumcision of newborn males.

In girls, I am looking for evidence of inflammation, because infection is common in girls. I never touch the genitalia in a girl. I get the mother to spread the labial lips, and I look with my exam light.

I check the bum hole in both girls and boys. I find poop that is not a wiping issue more common than mothers acknowledge. I always check for the "anal wink." This is a neurological test. When the child is up on his knees with his forehead on the table and his bum back, I stroke the bum skin a few inches from the bum hole. If the anus "winks" or closes in response, this confirms the nerve is intact both to and from the spinal cord.

Checking the underwear is often revealing. I look for the "three Ps"— poop, pee, and pus. If the underwear is damp at the front, this confirms daytime wetting is an issue. If there is pus at the front in a girl, infection is likely. This usually presents as a tiny string of pus that has been squeezed out over the length of the labia. Any more poop than a real skid mark should be considered soiling.

One colleague of mine had a good definition of the difference between a wiping issue (a real skid mark) and soiling.

"If you can scrape it, it's soiling."

I can finish the history, physical examination, urine test, and figure out the bladder size in about one and a quarter hours for most families. This usually leaves me forty-five minutes to explain the causes of bedwetting to the child and mother, to outline my recommendations, and to answer questions.

The next three chapters will outline how I cure bedwetting.

How to Cure Bedwetting

My goal is to cure bedwetting in every child, and I would like the child to be confidently dry on the best possible terms. This means the child should be dry and not need to restrict fluids in the evening, dry and not thirsty at bedtime, and he should be dry and be able to hydrate himself properly for evening sport activities or social occasions.

My treatment approach is properly referred to as behavioural health therapy.

When I first started to treat with and teach about this approach, I used the term *urotherapy*, which I learned from Professor Kelm Hjälmås, a Swedish urologist. Kelm was my mentor and friend. I learned more about how children pee from him than from any paper or textbook. He wrote many of the original papers on voiding in children.

European physicians understand what is meant by the word *urotherapy*, but this term is not well recognized in North America. Therefore, I used the term *behavioural therapy* in the United States and Canada. I continued to use this terminology until 2010, when my good friend Dr. Bill Warzak, a psychologist at the University of Wisconsin, corrected me on this important semantic point.

To my knowledge, I am the only person in the world to offer this comprehensive approach, but many good physicians around the world teach aspects of my approach.

The basic premise of my approach is that I want to cure bedwetting, and I do not want to use a medication to accomplish this.

I do not use medications to reduce overnight urine production or medications to increase how much the bladder can hold. These approaches do not cure. These approaches are not usually successful even as a control. They can also have side effects. In a later chapter, I will discuss these medications, why they don't work, and the common side effects.

The right way to cure bedwetting is to help the bladder to hold more, help the kidney to make enough pee to fit in the bladder, and help the brain to wake up the child when the bladder is full.

I can achieve this with a compliant child and cooperative family in six months. Some families take longer. There is no race to dryness. Every child and family should set a pace that works for their unique personal and family circumstances. I ask the families to assess their child and home situation and to be realistic about the process. I tell everyone that there is no such thing as a "quick fix" to cure bedwetting.

Having said that, I encourage children and families to work to achieve dryness as promptly as possible. When the project slows down, the child and family start to lose interest and motivation, and progress can stall.

Helping the Bladder to Hold More

Helping the bladder to hold more is mostly about improving the bowel health.

The goal is to achieve bladder-friendly bowel health.

I define this as a soft, mushy poop every morning after breakfast before the child leaves for school or before he starts his play day, great emptying, and a second poop later in the day on as many days as possible.

The time for a child to achieve this varies considerably, but if the child and family follow my recommendations carefully, this can be achieved in two months for some and four months for most. Some children achieve this in a month. Others never improve. Guess which ones were more disciplined, were more motivated, and followed the recommendations the most closely?

The Morning Poop

There is always poop in the rectum in the morning, and there is always a signal to poop after a meal. Breakfast is the morning meal, and there is always a signal after breakfast. Lots of parents tell me that they never have a signal in the morning. I respond, "You also don't usually notice that your heart is beating or that your lungs are breathing, but they are."

The signal is there, waiting to be acted upon.

First, the family needs to decide that the morning poop is essential. It is!

Every morning, there is poop in the rectum. After working on my recommendations, this poop will be ready, willing, and able to come out. If the child does not poop in the morning, then by definition the child is starting to withhold from the beginning of each day, and withholding is a key reason why the bowel health got worse in the first place.

When we poop and empty well in the morning, the pelvis is relatively free of poop for the morning and the bladder is able to hold more. The bladder needs to hold more by day to learn to hold more at night. I tell the parents that the bladder needs to practice holding more by day so that it can hold more at night. Although not proven, I suspect that how much the bladder holds by day sets a sort of "bladder stat," and the brain accepts this as the appropriate volume to empty at night.

When the bladder holds more by day, the child is more inclined to drink more during the day.

For children who have urgency and daytime wetting, the morning poop is even more important. Getting rid of the poop wall at the start of the day minimizes racing to the bathroom and dampness.

For the children who void exceptionally frequently, the attentive voiders, the morning poop is essential.

A good poop in the morning opens up the possibility of a second poop later in the day.

You cannot poop too often, if you want a bigger bladder.

Have I mentioned that the morning poop is very important?

Second, the family needs to change the morning routine to allow time for a morning poop. The child needs to get up early enough to have breakfast early enough, and there needs to be a full ten minutes to practice sitting on the toilet every morning.

This can be the biggest challenge for a family. Bobby is fairly typical. He needs his sleep; everyone in the family does. All the family members stay up later than they should, and they are all usually tired in the morning. Bobby is more tired on hockey nights and harder to wake up the next morning. Many mornings, his mother would prefer to let him sleep for another fifteen minutes. Whenever his mother does try to wake him, Bobby doesn't always want to get up with the first wake-up call. In Bobby's home, he usually has only forty-five minutes from the time he gets out of bed until he needs to walk to the bus. This is not enough time for a poop before he leaves for school. The poop is there. The signal arrives on time. But there is no time to pay attention to the signal. When the signal comes, Bobby, without knowing it, much like breathing, just tightens the pelvic floor muscles and pushes his pasty poop back up, postponing the event. He can do this really well. He has practiced this for most of his life.

I recommend that the family get Bobby up fifteen minutes earlier. They might need to consider an earlier bedtime. Perhaps Mom or Dad should consider driving him to school to save some of the time spent on the school bus.

If the family does not budget the extra time, Bobby will not achieve a morning poop.

Life often conspires against the best intentions of many families.

What if his mother is single and his two younger siblings are a handful to get ready every morning? Mom will not have enough time to encourage the morning poop, much less drive him to school.

What if both parents need to work to pay the mortgage? Perhaps Dad leaves for an early work shift so that he can come home to be there for the children, while Mom, who leaves two hours later, is still at work.

What if there is a new baby in the home, Mom was up all night nursing, and she needs to sleep in the next morning?

What if the parents are not getting along, and all their emotional energy goes into this struggle rather than into going the extra mile for Bobby?

What if Dad just lost his city job, and he is now working out of town—he sends money home, but he is away for weeks at a time and Mom is alone?

What if Bobby's parents are divorced and he spends half his time at his dad's and half at his mom's? And what if his dad is not as organized as his mom, or vice versa? What if his parents have remarried and there are stepparents and stepsiblings? How do these new family members affect the morning routines?

What if Mom runs a day home to help with the finances and the mothers often drop the children off before the expected time?

What if the car breaks down, someone gets sick, the in-laws visit, the weather is bad, or the dog needs to be taken to the vet?

What if …?

On the other hand, sometimes life conspires to help us out.

What if Bobby is an only child?

What if Mom does not work and has the luxury of driving him to school?

What if both parents work, but they work from home?

What if the family is very well off and there is a live-in nanny?

What if Bobby is homeschooled?

What if …?

Travel almost always affects bowel health. One Mom told me, "If I look at a suitcase, I don't poop for three days."

Other aspects of the morning routine might need to be changed. The child needs to have a designated bathroom to use after breakfast, and depending on the ratio of bathrooms to people, this can be a challenge.

One six-year-old girl I follow has yet to have a morning poop. Mom is single. There are four children. Sometimes her boyfriend stays over, and there is only one bathroom in the home. The girl has two older adolescent sisters, and they tie up the bathroom in the mornings. Mom drives a school bus and needs to get everyone up and out of the house early. Her daughter with the bedwetting eats breakfast on the school bus.

The designated bathroom should be quiet. If the child can hear the television or a sibling who is playing a video game, there is less chance the child will focus on a good poop.

The bathroom needs to be comfortable. In colder seasons, the bathrooms on the outside walls can be chilly. Most modern parents are energy-conservation conscious, so they turn down the temperature overnight. The child needs to be comfortable if the parents expect him to cooperate and sit for ten minutes on a cold winter morning.

The child needs to take something into the bathroom to help him relax and to keep him sitting there for a full ten minutes. A comic book, sports magazine, or an age-appropriate children's book are the common tools. Portable video games are okay if the child does not make the game a physical workout as he manipulates the buttons. The newer portable DVD players work for some younger children. Some early elementary–aged children can sit for a long time watching their favourite cartoon character. I generally recommend that a parent sit with preschool children for at least the first few weeks to encourage cooperation.

I know this is a huge challenge, but I also know that the morning poop is a key component of bladder-friendly bowel health. I also know that this can be achieved notwithstanding what would appear to be insurmountable obstacles.

I have witnessed many poop miracles in my office, and I know that children and families can achieve a morning poop if they really decide to do this.

I have a personal story to tell.

I have enjoyed bladder-friendly bowel health for as long as I can remember, and I have been telling people for years that this can be accomplished, even under difficult circumstances, so long as the individual follows the rules.

In the spring of 2010, I had an opportunity to test myself. I spent two weeks working as a disaster relief paediatrician in Haiti, and I worked in a very demanding environment. I had to be up early to get into a truck to travel to clinics. I was with other people who set the schedule and who routinely changed the schedule. I was not eating a diet even remotely similar to usual. I didn't trust the food and mostly ate energy bars. The temperature was so hot and the working environment so humid that I needed to drink four litres of water during the day. I was always concerned that the water was contaminated. Even though I did manage to drink this much over the workday, I never had to pee for the entire ten or twelve hours while I was at work! When you can go up to half a day without a signal for the need to pee, you are clearly behind on your fluid intake. When I did pee at the end of the day, my urine was always dark. Some of the bathroom facilities I used were disgusting beyond belief.

Well, I pooped every morning but one in that two weeks. I was determined to keep my routine, and I did. My diet changed, my hydration was poor, bathroom access was an issue, and I was often rushed in the morning. All in all, I think I proved my point.

So I not only talk the talk, I walk the walk.

For the record, my personal bathroom routine is to poop at least twice a day on weekdays and three times a day on weekends. I drink a litre of juice before I go to the office every morning. I pee about six or eight times over the course of a day.

So, it can be done.

As Christmas approaches, I get into the spirit of things and start singing Christmas carols, and as the children leave the office and I wish them a Merry Christmas, I sometimes ask them what they want from Santa. After they respond, I make another suggestion:

"All I want for Christmas
is a morning poop."

Another title for this chapter might be:

"Field of Poops: Sit and It Will Come."

Now, after deciding that the morning poop is a priority and after rearranging the morning logistics of the household, the next step is to work on emptying.

If the child poops every day but doesn't empty, this is very similar to not pooping at all. The poop wall remains.

Emptying

Emptying is, first of all, about posture. The child needs to sit in the middle of the toilet with the knees relaxed apart, and the feet need to be flat on either the floor or a platform. This posture emulates the natural squat and allows the pelvic floor muscles around the bum hole to optimally relax and allow the poop to come out.

Most children have learned to poop perched forward on the toilet with their knees held together and their feet dangling. This is by far the most common posture in girls. Another common posture is to hold the bum over the middle of the toilet with the hands on the sides of the toilet seat; boys do this more than girls. Children carry these postures with them as they age. Even once they are able to sit comfortably in the middle of the toilet without their bum sinking in, they often continue to keep their knees together. Emptying will not be optimal until the knees relax apart. If you need proof of this, the next time you are having a pasty, log-shaped poop, try moving your knees apart and together and feel the difference in how the poop comes out. You will find that when you move the knees together, the poops slows down and when you move the knees apart, the poop comes out easier. Many mothers in my office have an "aha" moment when I explain this. I know that I have improved the emptying of lots of parents.

Depending on the size of the toilet and the size of the bum, an over-the-toilet seat might be required. An over-the-toilet seat is generally required until the child is about six years of age, but some thin eight-year-olds might still need this convenience. The child needs to sit comfortably in the middle of the toilet without sinking in or holding on. Don't presume. Have your child sit in the middle of your toilet at home and check to be sure. The over-the-toilet seats I use in my office cost less than five dollars at Walmart. I suggest parents buy enough of these over-the-toilet seats so that there is one in every bathroom the child is likely to use. There are also regular adult toilet seats available with a built-in child-sized toilet that flips down.

Ideally, the pants and underwear should be off, so that there is nothing that will pull the knees together. The pants and underwear should at least be pulled down to the ankles. This is easy to accomplish at home, especially with the morning poop, since lots of children are still in their pyjamas. However, in a public washroom, this is not so simple. I don't know about you, but I'm not comfortable pulling my pants down to the ankles in a public toilet. The floors are gross!

Having said that, I can recollect numerous times in my life when I have seen a man's pants on the floor in a cubicle in a public toilet. Until I learned about the importance of posture, I presumed these men were stupid. Now I can clarify their stupidity. They are smart about posture, but not so smart about hygiene.

The feet need to be flat on either the floor or a platform. Unless a child is very tall for his age, his feet will not rest flat on the floor while he is sitting on a conventional home toilet until he is about eight years old. I recommend that the child use a stool, a phone book wrapped up in duct tape, some two-by-six pieces of wood, or a pile of larger coffee table–sized books that you don't mind getting pee on. There are a variety of different heights of stools available. Rubbermaid makes a higher stool, and IKEA sells a lower stool. The feet should be flat.

At the first visit to my office, I review the posture with the child. For girls and for boys who sit to pee, I review this when they pee in the Uroflow toilet after the ultrasound. I sit on a chair and demonstrate the desired posture. I have four different height stools in the bathroom and some medical texts of varying width. After explaining about the posture and the need for flat feet, I ask the mothers to choose the appropriate stool and to add books as necessary to achieve the desired posture.

In medical school, I acquired a reputation for buying a lot of books. Sometimes, when I tell the parents to use the books to achieve the right posture, I smile and say, "And some of my friends told me I'd never use these books."

After posture, the next important emptying principle is to relax and sit still. Having a book or a portable video game helps. Some children never sit still. Children with ADHD might have a problem with this. Practice makes perfect, and these children need personal trainers, otherwise known as parents.

Never rush and never push are the final rules of great emptying. If the child is in a rush, he doesn't empty. Pushing interferes with emptying.

Once the child has achieved bladder-friendly bowel health, a morning poop without pushing should take five minutes from start to finish. From the time he gets the signal to the time he has emptied, wiped, and washed his hands, it should take about five minutes. However, at the start, I recommend that every child sit for ten minutes by the clock. Some children need a clock to help them learn how long ten minutes really is. This is a variation of the "Are we there yet?" sense of time. If the child is in and out of the bathroom in one or two minutes, the parent should presume the child did not empty.

Many children would like to follow the rules, and what they hear is that a morning poop is needed. So they sit, push out a small piece, flush, and run to tell Mom how well they have done. I recommend that parents monitor the morning poop. Pushing out a small, pasty piece is not emptying and is not bladder-friendly bowel health. The poop wall persists in this situation.

One of my all-time favourite responses to my question about how long a child sat on the toilet was the parent who replied, "Not long. I don't think the seat gets warm."

From the start, I ask children to sit every morning without fail for ten minutes and to keep doing this until they start having morning poops. I tell them that depending on how quickly their poop softens up, they might have to sit for weeks or even months before the morning poops start. If they sit and don't poop after breakfast, I ask them to sit again after lunch on weekends and holidays and after school and supper on school days. On the way to achieving a morning poop, achieving a poop each day is an important intermediate step.

I tell the children:

Come what may,
you need a poop a day.

A variation on this for the children who keep coming back without progress is:

A poop a day
keeps Dr. Lane away.

I don't ask children to try to poop at school, but if they need to and are prepared to, that is fine. I don't recommend a school poop because children don't empty well at school. The child will not spend enough time and will not have good posture, so emptying will be compromised. Some parents return for a follow-up and report that their child is pooping every morning at school. Some might be. But some are telling their parents what they want to hear and the parents are hearing what they want to hear. The goal should be a morning poop at home, not at school.

Some children only achieve morning poops on weekends, and of course, this means the home is too rushed or the logistics have not otherwise been set up to achieve success on school days.

Once a child has achieved a morning poop with great emptying, a second poop later in the day becomes more and more common if the child chooses to respond to signals and there is good access to a bathroom.

Now, the softer the stool, the easier it is to make the transition to a morning poop with great emptying. Generally, unless the poop changes from hard and pasty to soft and mushy, the pattern will not change. So, soft, mushy poop is essential.

Soft, Mushy Stool

Soft stool is mostly about hydration. The poop will not be soft if the hydration is poor.

Soft stool is also about diet. There are foods that make the poop soft and foods that make the poop hard.

Fibre helps make the poop soft. There needs to be sufficient fibre in every meal and snack to hold the moisture in the poop.

About once a month, a mother tells me her child's poop must be perfect. "The poop must be perfect. He has more fibre in his diet than anyone I know." But the ultrasound tells a different story. There might well be lots of fibre in the diet, but without water, the poop will still be hard or pasty. About once a year, a mother who is also a dietician comes in, and these moms are often quite perplexed about why the poop in their child is so hard. These mothers have actually counted the grams of fibre in their child's diet, and they know he is getting lots. Fibre is great, but again, without water, the poop will still be hard or pasty.

I recommend 25 grams of fibre a day for a child between the ages of four and ten years. Adults should have 35 grams a day. I suggest starting the day with oatmeal with raisins or some other dried fruit, such as apricots, or with fresh fruit. I also recommend lots of fruits and vegetables. There should be a fruit or vegetable with every meal and snack. I recommend that a child have *eight grams of fibre with each meal*. This allows at least 24 grams of fibre a day.

The tables on the next pages show the fibre content of some common foods. There is no fibre in meat or dairy. The data comes from the 2010 edition of *Bowes and Church's Food Values of Portions Commonly Used*.[7] Within each food category, the high fibre foods are at the top of each group.

---

7   Jean A. T. Pennington and Judith Spungen Wolters, *Bowes and Church's Food Values of Portions Commonly Used*, Wolters Kluwer/Lippincott Williams & Wilkins (2010).

Food		Quantity	Grams
Breakfast Cereals			
All Bran Buds	Kellogg's	1 cup	39.1
All Bran	Kellogg's	1 cup	18.2
Alpen	Weetabix	1 cup	10.3
Raison Bran	Kellogg's	1 cup	6.5
Oat Bran Flakes	Kellogg's	1 cup	5.2
oatmeal	quick regular	1 cup	4.0
Just Right	Fruit & Nut Kellogg's	1 cup	3.1
Cheerios	Regular General Mills	1 cup	3.0
oatmeal	Quaker Honey Nut	1 packet	2.8
oatmeal	Quaker Apple Cinnamon	1 packet	2.7
oatmeal	Quaker Raison and Spice	1 packet	2.6
oatmeal	Quaker Fruit Cream	1 packet	2.0
Puffed Wheat	Kellogg's	1 cup	1.8
Froot Loops	Kellogg's	1 cup	0.9
Cap'n Crunch	Quaker	1 cup	0.9
Frosted Flakes	Kellogg's	1 cup	0.8
Corn Flakes	Kellogg's	1 cup	0.8
Special K	Kellogg's	1 cup	0.7
Rice Krispies	Kellogg's	1 cup	0.3

Bread, Pasta, Rice			
Bread, Pasta, Rice			
rice	brown, long-grain boiled	1 cup	3.5
rice	white, long-grain boiled	1 cup	1.0
pasta	spaghetti, whole wheat	1 cup	6.3
pasta	macaroni, whole wheat	1 cup	3.9
pasta	macaroni	1 cup	2.5
pasta	spaghetti	1 cup	2.5
bread	whole wheat	1 slice	1.9
bread	white	1 slice	0.6
bagel	oat bran	1	3.8
muffin	oat bran	1	6.4

Fruit			
blackberries		1 cup	15.2
avocado		1 cup	9.8
apricots	dried	1 medium	9.4
raspberries		1 cup	8.0
raisins	golden seedless	1 cup	5.8
papaya		1 medium	5.5
pear		1 medium	5.1
cranberries	dried	1 cup	3.8
mango		1 medium	3.7
blueberries		1 cup	3.5
apple		1 medium	3.3
banana		1 medium	3.1
orange		1 medium	3.1
strawberries		1 cup	2.9
dates		4	2.6
grapefruit		1 medium	2.6
cherries		1 cup	2.5
nectarine		1 medium	2.3
kiwifruit		1 medium	2.3
pineapple		1 cup	2.2
cantaloupe		1 cup	1.6
peach		1 medium	1.5
honeydew		1 cup	1.4
prunes		2	1.1
plum		1 medium	0.9
watermelon		1 cup	0.6

Nuts			
almonds	raw	1 oz	3.4
pistachios	dried	1 oz	2.9
pecans	dried	1 oz	2.7
peanut butter	chunky	2 tbs (1 oz)	2.6
coconut	raw	1 oz	2.5
peanuts	raw	1 oz	2.4
peanut butter	smooth	2 tbs (1 oz)	1.9
cashews	raw	1 oz	0.9

Vegetables			
popcorn	air popped	3.5 cups	4.1
green snap beans	raw	1 cup	3.7
potato	mashed	1 cup	3.6
corn	frozen	1 cup	3.4
brussels sprouts	raw	1 cup	3.3
okra	raw	1 cup	3.2
asparagus	raw	1 cup	2.8
cauliflower	raw	1 cup	2.5
sweet pepper	red raw	1 medium	2.5
broccoli	raw	1 cup	2.4
carrot	raw	1 medium	2.0
snow peas	raw	1 cup	1.6
cabbage, red	raw	1 cup	1.5
cucumber	raw	1 large	1.5
lettuce	iceberg	1 cup	0.7
spinach	raw	1 cup	0.7
tomato	raw	1 cup	0.7
celery	raw	1 medium	0.6

Beans, Lentils			
navy beans	boiled	1 cup	19.1
lentils	boiled	1 cup	15.6
kidney beans	boiled	1 cup	13.1
chickpeas	boiled	1 cup	12.5
soybeans	boiled	1 cup	10.3
lima beans	boiled	1 cup	9.0
green peas	boiled	1 cup	8.8

Dairy products and anything with a high fat content make the poop hard.

Dairy products are a major cause of hard poop. Dairy includes milk, cheese, and ice cream. Dairy is, first of all, a big problem because the children or their parents choose milk over juice or water. Milk is great for calories but terrible for hydration. I suggest that parents consider milk as a solid.

Milk is great for calories, but *terrible* for hydration.

Milk has fat, protein, carbohydrates, and lots of vitamins and minerals— all good for nutrition—but the body uses the water content of milk to process all the chemicals so there is not much water left over for the kidneys. Milk has fat content, even skim milk, and fat slows down the time it takes the food to move through the bowel. Fat slows down the transit time. Anything fatty does this, including dairy products.

Some parents ask if bedwetting can be caused by an allergy to cow's milk. The answer is no. Children who eat and drink a lot of dairy usually have hard and pasty poop, and this has an effect on bladder volume and function, but this is not an allergy.

Some parents ask if they should take dairy out of the diet. For some parents who seem genuinely interested in this topic, I respond with a quote from Dr. Benjamin Spock:

"Cow's milk is for cows."

Dr. Ben Spock was the author of the most popular baby book during the middle of the twentieth century. His book was the bible for the mothers of the baby boomers. Ben was an outspoken critic of cow's milk, as was Dr. Frank Oski. Dr. Oski was a professor of paediatrics at Johns Hopkins, and he was a star in the American paediatric academic world. Dr. Oski wrote a book entitled *Don't Drink Your Milk*. Together, he and Ben started a public awareness campaign to reduce cows' milk consumption. Ben and Dr. Oski pointed out that a cow's milk allergy is present in 1 to 2 per cent of children and that cow's milk intolerance is present in up to 60 per cent of individuals depending on race and age. They also pointed out the variety of problems that cow's milk has been linked to, including new reports that suggest a link with some cases of juvenile diabetes mellitus. I supported their position in letters to the editor of various medical and news publications.

Clearly, cow's milk is not healthy for some children. There are other sources for the nutrition available in cow's milk, and parents who are willing can achieve great nutrition without cow's milk.

When I was a young paediatric physician in training at Sick Kids in Toronto, there were two stereotypical groups of overweight toddlers who were still drinking from a bottle. One group arrived at the clinic with a bottle of milk dangling from the mouth. The other arrived with a bottle of juice. One group drank almost exclusively milk, and lots of milk. The other group drank almost exclusively juice, and lots of juice. The ones with the bottle of milk had hard, pasty poops and were often constipated. The ones with the juice had soft, mushy poops. Both groups had a lot of dental caries.

As a young paediatrician, I saw and helped many children with what was referred to as "toddler's diarrhoea." These were the juice-drinking children. They drank so much full-strength juice that they were overweight from the calories, they had dental caries, and they had mushy poop. The poop was not watery, just exceptionally soft and mushy, and the children usually had two and sometimes three poops a day. The parents were worried that there was some horrible kind of parasite or disease present to cause the "diarrhoea." This was not diarrhoea; this was normal poop! The main focus of concern for these children should have been their obesity and their dental health. The suggested treatment for these children was to drink more milk and less juice, and to add fat to the diet. I didn't like adding fat to the diet of an overweight baby, but the poops did firm up.

Great hydration leads to soft poops, morning movements, and great emptying.

So, what is great hydration?

The chart shows what I recommend for hydration for children of different weights.

Hydration (water and juice, not milk) per Day by Weight

weight pounds	weight kg	ml per day	ml before lunch	oz per day	oz before lunch
20	9.1	905	362	30	12
22.5	10.2	1010	404	34	13
25	11.4	1070	428	36	14
27.5	12.5	1125	450	38	15
30	13.6	1180	472	39	16
32.5	14.8	1240	496	41	17
35	15.9	1295	518	43	17
37.5	17.0	1350	540	45	18
40	18.2	1410	564	47	19
42.5	19.3	1465	586	49	20
45	20.5	1510	604	50	20
47.5	21.6	1532	613	51	20
50	22.7	1554	622	52	21
52.5	23.9	1578	631	53	21
55	25.0	1600	640	53	21
57.5	26.1	1622	649	54	22
60	27.3	1646	658	55	22
62.5	28.4	1668	667	56	22
65	29.5	1690	676	56	23
67.5	30.7	1714	686	57	23
70	31.8	1736	694	58	23
72.5	33.0	1760	704	59	23
75	34.1	1782	713	59	24
77.5	35.2	1804	722	60	24
80	36.4	1828	731	61	24
82	37.3	1846	738	62	25
82.5	37.5	1850	740	62	25
85	38.6	1872	749	62	25
87.5	39.8	1896	758	63	25
90	40.9	1918	767	64	26
92.5	42.0	1940	776	65	26
95	43.2	1964	786	65	26
97.5	44.3	1986	794	66	26
100	45.5	2010	804	67	27
102.5	46.6	2032	813	68	27
105	47.7	2054	822	68	27

Most children who wet the bed drink about half of the recommended amount on a routine day, and some much less. Those who drink more than half are mostly drinking late in the day. I recommend that the child drink 40 per cent of the recommended amount before lunch. Children need to "catch up" with their hydration every morning.

Drinking more is a real challenge for most of the children, and I don't recommend large, abrupt increases in the fluid intake. Instead, I recommend that the amount be slowly increased.

The table below shows how I suggest the amounts might be increased each week over three months for an eight-year-old boy like Bobby. At the start, the boy only has four ounces of milk at breakfast and a six-ounce juice box at lunch at school and then arrives home thirsty and starts to drink. The evening intake is much more on a sports night. Over three months, the boy will reach the recommended amount and pattern for his age.

	Breakfast	A.M. school	Lunch	P.M. school	Home	Supper	Evening	Total
Now	4		6		12	12	8	42
Week 1	6	4	6	4	8	12	8	42
2	6	4	6	4	8	12	8	42
3	6	4	6	4	8	12	8	42
4	6	4	6	4	8	12	8	42
5	8	6	6	6	8	12	8	46
6	8	6	6	6	8	12	8	46
7	8	6	6	6	8	12	8	46
8	8	6	6	6	8	12	8	46
9	10	8	6	8	8	12	8	50
10	10	8	6	8	8	12	8	50
11	10	12	6	8	8	12	8	54
12	10	12	6	8	8	12	8	54

Parents have some control over how much a child drinks before he leaves for school and after he arrives home, but they have little control while the child is at school. I recommend that the parents encourage the child to have a drink as soon as he gets up and again during breakfast. They should send a water bottle and clarify how much the boy should drink during the morning at school. Children find it very hard to hydrate well at school. The adage, "You can lead a horse to water, but you can't make him drink," might just as well apply to most schoolchildren.

To achieve bladder-friendly bowel health in a reasonable time frame, I recommend a stool softener as well as good hydration. Changing the diet to reduce dairy and to achieve the optimal amount of fibre can be a struggle. Many children like to eat what they enjoy, and some are picky eaters at the best of times. Changing the diet at the start of therapy can be an insurmountable obstacle for many families.

With a stool softener and good hydration, a child can achieve some morning poops within the first four to six weeks and a consistent routine with bladder-friendly bowel health within two to four months.

Some families can achieve the necessary softness without a stool softener. Every child who comes to my office can improve his bowel health, but some arrive with a pattern that is much closer to bladder-friendly bowel health than others. These children arrive with a story of more frequent poops, a diet with more fibre, and better hydration than the average. Their ultrasound images show a narrower rectum and stool that is usually just pasty.

I differentiate stool softeners from laxatives. Stool softeners only make the poop soft. They do not cause the bowels to move. Laxatives cause the bowels to move.

I don't recommend laxatives. Common laxatives include Dulcolax (bisacodyl) and Sennakot (extract of senna).

I also do not recommend enemas. I can almost always improve the bowel health without the need for these emotionally and physically traumatic interventions. Children might tolerate the first enema because they do not really know what to expect. Afterwards, they cannot believe that their parents would inflict this bum pain on them, and they generally don't cooperate with subsequent enemas.

When children have had enemas, I usually ask the parent how the child tolerated the procedure. The best (worst) story I've heard was from a dad who told me, "The first time we gave him an enema, we managed to get the tube in his bum, but since then, giving him an enema has been like trying to get a cat in a bath."

I do recommend stool softeners. I specifically recommend stool softeners that hold moisture in the bowel and therefore soften the stool naturally. The stool softeners I recommend include Polyethylene Glycol 3350 (Lax A Day or RestoraLAX in Canada and Miralax in the United States), Lactulose, Metamucil (psyllium), Fibersure (inulin), and Benefibre (inulin). I don't recommend the oily stool softeners like mineral oil.

Lactulose has been around for a long time. This is a large carbohydrate molecule that holds moisture in the bowel with an osmotic effect. Lactulose works the same way prune juice does. Both Lactulose and prune juice work fine, but many children do not prefer the taste of these softeners.

Metamucil, Fibersure, and Benefibre are fibre supplements, and these work well for some children.

My favourite is Lax A Day (RestoraLAX). Even though the name includes "Lax," this is not a true laxative; Lax A Day does not cause the bowels to move. The people who market this know that people equate "lax" with pooping, and the name therefore makes good marketing sense from their perspective. However, the name is terrible from my perspective. Every day, I have to explain why Lax A Day is not a true laxative that makes the bowels move. Lax a Day is an over-the-counter product in Canada and the United States. It is a tasteless powder that is mixed in with what a child drinks at meals. The tasteless nature is a big selling feature for me. The powder is a large chemical with a terrible sounding name—polyethylene glycol. This is not an organic product, and many parents desire an organic remedy. One parent told me she equated the Lax A Day to "eating plastic." I wish the product had a different name and was organic, but that is not the case. What I do know is that Lax A Day works and that the side effect profile is excellent. I have used Lax A Day for over a decade, and I have only had one child develop what I consider to be a genuine allergic reaction and one other child with a possible allergic reaction, and I have read about one other child with an allergic reaction. From my perspective, this is a safe stool softener. The chemical that softens the stool does so by holding moisture in the bowel, and the chemical is not absorbed into the body. The chemical is pooped out in the stool and not retained in the body, which explains why the risk of an allergic reaction is so low. I use Lax A Day from the time a child is able to drink from a bottle or a cup.

I know children can achieve soft, mushy poop with hydration and a stool softener; I leave it up to the parents to decide whether they prefer to change the diet or which poop softener to use, but most of the parents in my clinic choose Lax A Day. The bottom line is to achieve a soft, mushy morning poop in a reasonable period of time, say two to four months.

The only real side effect with any poop softener is if the poop becomes too soft. The child may try to hold in poop that is too soft or think he is passing gas and poop comes out. Soiling is common if you don't follow the rules with poop softeners. I tell all the children, "Don't guess with gas."

Start low and go slow.

My rule is to start with a very low dose and to increase the dose slowly.

Go up slowly enough, perhaps increasing the dose every one or two weeks, so that the child has time to learn what the poop feels like as the stool changes from hard to pasty to soft to mushy. All the children are familiar with hard and pasty poop. They are well practiced in the art of holding in hard and pasty poop. They have no experience with soft and mushy poop, and unless they get a chance to practice, accidents will happen. So, start low and go slow. If a parent and child are prepared to be very attentive to the change in stool consistency, they can increase the dose every week. If a parent and child are not likely to be as attentive, they should increase the dose every two weeks. If a child already has a problem with soiling, I always recommend that the dose be increased as slowly as necessary.

I calculate the average dose of Lax A Day for the weight of the child, and I divide this by three to split the amount between breakfast, lunch, and supper. Then I take a quarter of the average dose for a meal, and that is where I suggest the parent start. So, this is a very low dose. Every week or two, the dose should be increased by about ¼ teaspoon. The average dose for an eight-year-old is usually about 1½ to 2 teaspoons with each meal. To start low, I usually start at ½ teaspoon, and every one or two weeks, I increase the dose by ¼ teaspoon. So, the dose would go from ½ teaspoon to ¾ teaspoon, to 1 teaspoon, to 1¼ teaspoon, and so on until the poop softens enough that a morning routine can be established. Once a morning routine is established, the parent can consider stopping at that dose. Unless the bowel health is really terrible, the child hardly ever requires the average dose for weight.

The table on the next page shows the average dose per day for children of various weights. The last column shows the average dose for breakfast, lunch, and supper.

Average Dose of Lax A Day by Weight

lbs	kg	Total Teaspoons per Day	Teaspoons at Breakfast, Lunch, & Supper
20	9.1	2.4	0.8
22.5	10.2	2.7	0.9
25	11.4	3.0	1.0
27.5	12.5	3.3	1.1
30	13.6	3.6	1.2
32.5	14.8	3.9	1.3
35	15.9	4.2	1.4
37.5	17.0	4.5	1.5
38	17.3	4.6	1.5
40	18.2	4.8	1.6
42.5	19.3	5.2	1.7
45	20.5	5.5	1.8
47.5	21.6	5.8	1.9
50	22.7	6.1	2.0
52.5	23.9	6.4	2.1
55	25.0	6.7	2.2
57.5	26.1	7.0	2.3
60	27.3	7.3	2.4
62.5	28.4	7.6	2.5
65	29.5	7.9	2.6
67.5	30.7	8.2	2.7
70	31.8	8.5	2.8

Regularly, I will have parents come in and report that their child is still not pooping every day and that the poop, while softer, is still pasty. They are perplexed because they have slowly increased the stool softener to the average dose and the pattern has not improved as much as they had hoped. This invariably means the child has not improved his hydration. You can have optimal fibre in your diet or the average dose of stool softener, but unless there is enough water intake, the poop will stay pasty.

Recently I saw a child who proves this point. A mom brought in a five-year-old girl with constipation, soiling, and bedwetting. Mom was mostly concerned about the constipation and soiling, and for good reason. The problems with constipation started when the child was about two years old, and her current pattern was to pass a very painful poop once a week and otherwise have substantial soilings almost every day. This was such a problem that the mom did not send her child to kindergarten. The first appointment was in June, and the mom was frantic about the forthcoming start of grade one. Mom was single, but there was a dad in the picture who helped out with child care on some evenings and weekends. Dad did not work. The only source of income was Mom, who ran a day home. The little girl had an attentive bladder personality. She voided frequently but did not wet by day. I discussed bladder-friendly bowel health with Mom, and when she left, her eyes confirmed she was on a mission. She returned two months later in August.

"Thank you," she started out. "Within two weeks, she was pooping every day and the soiling stopped. Within another week, she was pooping every morning. Now she poops twice a day."

"Wonderful," I replied. "Congratulations."

She changed her tone and went on.

"But I'm sorry, Dr. Robson. I never started the stool softener."

"That's okay," I replied. "You're doing great."

She clarified, "I couldn't afford to buy the Lax A Day."

"No matter, whatever works, works," I responded. "What did you do to ensure the poop was soft enough?" I asked.

"Well," she replied, "you told me to have her drink fifty ounces a day and twenty ounces before lunch, so I had her drink seventy ounces a day, and thirty ounces before lunch. I also increased the fibre in her diet."

This is a great story, but this would not be possible in most homes. The mom was home all day with her daughter, so she could spend all the time necessary to encourage her to drink, and the daughter was especially compliant. The daughter will turn six and start grade one in the fall, and so long as she continues to poop and empty every morning, she will likely be fine without soiling. However, she will certainly not hydrate as well when she is on her own at school, and this could lead to a relapse.

Another stool softener rule is to take the softener with every meal. This ensures that all poop ends up soft at the bottom end. Each meal needs hydration and either lots of fibre—and I mean lots—or a stool softener. I consider the stool softener as a "fibre substitute." Parents often do not give the stool softener with the lunch meal at school because it requires extra effort and time to mix the softener in a container of juice and to include this in the lunch. I recommend the few extra minutes of effort, especially if cheese, milk, or meat figure prominently in the lunch. The instructions from the manufacturer of Lax A Day recommend a once-a-day dose, but I always ask the parents to give some with every major meal and even with big snacks.

Hard poop is compact logs or balls, and sinks with a clunk.

You need to get past paste.

Pasty poop is log-shaped and looks soft to many parents but really isn't. It keeps the shape as the stool sinks and is flushed. I have a problem with paste. Pasty poop is pokey poop. Pasty poop will not cooperate to settle into place when a child sits after breakfast, does not empty easily, and encourages the child to push, which is counterproductive. I tell parents that their child needs to get "past paste." The goal is mushy poop.

The magic is in the mush.

Mushy poop is the ultimate bladder-friendly poop. The magic is in the mush. Mushy poop settles easily into place—no pushing required. Mushy poop breaks apart as the stool sinks and flushes. Mushy poop is a pile on the floor of the toilet. A cow patty is mushy poop. These herbivores have great poop. Ironically, the animals that have the perfect mushy poop produce the milk that hardens human poop.

Parents sometimes ask me, "When will I know the poop is mushy?" Of course they can see for themselves if the child doesn't flush and they choose to look, so this is what I recommend. They will also know they are on the right course when the child has established a great morning routine without pushing.

Sometimes I feel a bit mischievous when I'm asked this question, and I reply:

"The proof is in the pudding."

Ugh! My youngest daughter would call that a gross "knee-slapper."

Speaking of knee-slappers, children love toilet humour, and so do many parents. I have the greatest job in the world for pee and poop jokes and for pee and poop puns. I try to make every child smile and laugh with each visit. I'm big into Dr. Seuss–style rhymes, as are the children.

> Talking about pee and pooh,
> makes it easy for me and you.

When they are walking into the Uroflow room to pee, I sometimes call out:

> Show me the pee!

Or, when they are climbing onto the ultrasound table, I say:

> We'll take a peek at your pee,
> then show you the pooh.

I could go on forever.

Now you know how to achieve bladder-friendly bowel health. This is one of three things you need to do to cure bedwetting. Once the child achieves a mushy morning poop with great emptying and a second poop on some days, you will know because he will stop running to the bathroom, the daytime wetting and dampness will fade away, and he will have daytime control for perhaps the first time in his life. Wow! That alone is worth the effort to achieve bladder-friendly bowel health.

You will also start to realize that the bladder of your child can hold more during the day. He will be drinking more, but peeing less often at school, or you will make that trip to the cottage and not need to stop for him to pee. You will go to a movie, and he can drink a soda and you will not have to take him to the bathroom during the most exciting part. You need to look for these signs as subjective evidence that the daytime bladder capacity has improved. This will confirm you are on the right track because if a bladder can hold more by day, the bladder can hold more at night.

The next pages are the hand-out on bladder-friendly bowel health that parents take home from my office.

Bladder-Friendly Bowel Health

The bladder and the bowel are side-by-side at the bottom of the pelvis where there is not much room. When children do not poop every day, when they do not empty well when they do poop, and when the poop is hard, the bladder is squished. There is a wall of poop around the bladder.

Once the bladder is full and up against the **POOP WALL**, there is no more room to expand, and the children either suddenly need to run to the bathroom or they wet. The **POOP WALL** makes the bladder hold less pee than normal.

The optimal bladder-friendly bowel pattern is for a child to have a poop after breakfast and before leaving for school, for the child to always empty well when pooping, and for the poop to be so soft and mushy that the bladder can push the poop out of the way as necessary to expand and hold more. A second poop later in the day is even more bladder friendly.

All people can poop in the morning if they decide to do so and follow some basic rules. There is always poop waiting to come out in the morning, and there is a signal of the need to poop after every meal. Whenever we eat, the body tries to empty to make room. Everyone learns to ignore (manage) signals to fit in with his or her personal schedules.

The child needs to sit on the toilet for ten minutes every morning after breakfast. The child needs to sit even if he or she does not have any signal of the need to poop. The child needs to take this time to practice sitting at the right time.

The child needs to be up early enough to have breakfast and to have the ten minutes to sit without being rushed. Most children need to wake up one hour before they leave for school to accomplish a morning poop. Sometimes the family needs to revise the entire home schedule to accomplish this.

The child needs access to a bathroom without siblings who compete for access. He or she needs a quiet, focused environment without noisy distractions outside. If there is a video game or TV on in the next room, the child will likely not relax and focus on the poop. In the colder winter months, the bathroom should be warm. Children need a book, magazine, or toy to keep them occupied. For preschool children, the parents should sit with them.

The child needs optimal posture to relax the pelvic floor muscles for good emptying. The optimal posture emulates the squat, which is the natural position to poop. The child needs to sit in the middle of the toilet without holding on to the sides. Preschool children need an over-the-toilet seat so that they can sit comfortably in the middle without sinking in. The knees need to be spread apart, which means the pants and underwear should be off. The feet need to be flat on the floor or a stool. Choose a stool or platform that allows the child to sit in the middle with the knees horizontal to the ground and not pushed up high above the toilet seat. Sitting should be comfortable.

Once sitting in the optimal posture, the child needs to consciously relax. Taking a deep breath and breathing out slowly (a yoga manoeuvre) can help the child to relax.

Pushing does not help. Pushing results in some poop coming out, but as the pelvic floor muscles contract to push, these muscles also cut off the poop and push some back in. With good bowel health, pushing should not be necessary.

Soft poop makes all the difference. Great hydration and a poop softener are necessary to achieve a daily morning routine with good emptying and soft poop.

Lax A Day (RestoraLAX, Miralax in the United States, polyethylene glycol) is the poop softener I recommend. This poop softener is safe, tasteless, and works well. *The poop softener is mixed into what the child drinks with breakfast, lunch, and dinner and holds water as the food is turned into poop.* The poop softener is not absorbed into the body; it is pooped out and is not retained in the body. Lax A Day is an over-the-counter medication and is therefore judged very safe by the government authorities that regulate medications.

A teaspoon of Lax A Day mixes well in eight oz of any fluid; half a teaspoon mixes well in four oz.

I recommend that the dose be started very low and increased slowly so the child has time to learn how to pay attention to the signals as the poop changes from hard or pasty to soft and mushy. If the poop changes to mush too quickly, the child will have accidents because he or she is not used to paying attention to the signals of soft poop. The child will presume the signal is gas. I recommend that the dose be increased every week or two until the stool is soft and mushy and the pattern changes to pooping every morning.

Pasty poop looks soft to most parents, but this poop is not soft enough. Pasty poop does not settle into place when you sit in the morning; pasty poop does not result in a good signal in the morning; pasty poop does not empty well; and pasty poop encourages pushing.

The goal is mushy poop. Mushy poop comes out as a log but breaks apart as it sinks and breaks apart more as it flushes. Mushy poop does not keep the log shape and is usually a pile on the bottom of the toilet.

Lax A Day Dose
The average dose based on your child's weight is __ tsp three times a day at breakfast, lunch, and supper.
Start with __ tsp three times a day.
Increase this every one or two weeks to __ tsp, then __ tsp, then __ tsp, and so on until the poop is soft and mushy and the pattern changes to a morning routine and then stay at that dose.

Lax A Day is safe to take for a long time.
The goal is take the Lax A Day long enough to for the bladder or bowel symptoms to resolve and for the child to build a great daily routine and to normalize his or her hydration and improve the fibre in his or her diet. Once this is accomplished, the Lax A Day is usually easy to stop without relapse.

Five years ago, when I opened up my current practice and devoted my time exclusively to helping children with bedwetting, I started off trying to cure bedwetting not only without a medication but also without a bedwetting alarm. Several years ago, I realized this was a poor approach. I learned that the daytime bladder capacity and control improves much faster than the nighttime bladder capacity and control. Children were not running to the bathroom and were dry by day, but night dryness was not improving very fast.

My sense is that the nighttime bladder capacity improves about a half an ounce a month once bladder-friendly bowel health is achieved. For Bobby, who is starting off with a bladder that only holds three ounces and who will be dry when his bladder holds about ten ounces, the difference is seven ounces; based on my estimate, Bobby might need fourteen months to achieve dryness. This is a very long time.

I learned that many families lose momentum and progress stalls as time drags on.

I also learned that alarms speed up the process, but that bladder-friendly bowel health was an important prerequisite for successful alarm therapy. The reasons for this will be discussed in the chapter on alarm therapy.

So, now I talk about and consider plans for alarm therapy from the very first appointment. At the first visit, I suggest to the family that we could start alarm therapy in two or four months, depending on when they believe they can realistically achieve bladder-friendly bowel health. I started giving the child and the parents a realistic goal, and this helped. Many families have responded, and now I graduate more children and in a shorter period of time.

For many years, I gave a basic talk on bedwetting. The title of the talk was "Paving the Road to Dryness," and this is precisely what children are doing when they work on bladder-friendly bowel health and hydration prior to the start of alarm therapy.

Next, we will discuss what to do if bladder infection is part of the bladder-capacity problem.

But before I forget, have I told you how important it is to poop in the morning?

Stop the Bladder Infection

Bladder infection (cystitis) is a part of the bedwetting problem in about 10 per cent of the children, and almost all of these are girls. Sometimes the parents already know about the infection, and sometimes the first visit to my office is when they learn about it.

A bladder that is infected with bacteria will not hold as much; the bladder will empty at a smaller volume than usual for the age and size of the child.

Sometimes the relationship between bladder infection and wetting is crystal clear. The mother reports that the nighttime wetting coincides with episodes of well-recognized infection, and the nighttime wetting resolves when the infection is successfully treated with an antibiotic.

Other times, the presence of the infection is totally unrecognized and has been ongoing literally for years!

Bedwetting is a well-recognized symptom of bladder infection. Other common symptoms include voiding more often (frequency), running to the bathroom (urgency), daytime wetting, discomfort with voiding, and an odour to the urine. When there is also fresh blood in the urine and the child has lower abdominal cramps with peeing, this is referred to as hemorrhagic cystitis.

If there is a fever and the child feels generally unwell, as with poor appetite, tiredness, nausea, and vomiting, this suggests the infection is also in the kidney (pyelonephritis). Kidney infection is a more serious problem than bladder infection but is not a cause of bedwetting and will not be discussed in this book. The only point about kidney infection that I will make is that kidney infection happens when bacteria from the bladder find their way up a ureter tube to the kidney. The most common reason why this happens is because the bladder muscle does not close off the hole where the ureter tube enters the bladder. If this hole doesn't close, some of the urine in the bladder is pushed up to the kidney. This is referred to as reflux, and the most common cause of acquired reflux is constipation. Kidney infection equals reflux equals the bowel health needs work.

The bacteria that cause bladder infection almost always originate in the bowel. They come out with the poop. These bacteria find their way to the genital area, and depending on how good or poor a child is with personal hygiene, there might be a little or a lot of bacteria in the genital area. When there are a lot of bacteria, this can cause irritation and itching, and if the mother looks at the genital area at this time, the labia and the area between the labia will usually be red and inflamed. There might be an odour as well. The colour between the labia should be a light pink, like the colour of your nail beds. If the area is red and inflamed, the child might experience some discomfort with voiding when the warm urine flows over the reddened areas between the labia. The chemical effects of retained pee behind the labia, the effects of chronic dampness, and trauma from itching and rubbing the area can also cause redness. A green or yellow discharge suggests well-established infection with bacteria in the genital area.

I am amazed at how poor the genital hygiene is in many girls. The parents are not to blame. No one has taught them what to do or what to look for. We have all grown up with advice to brush our teeth after every meal, but no one suggests rinsing the genitalia even once a day. Go figure.

Perhaps parents are victims of the "don't touch that" and "don't talk about that" prudishness that is presumed to be a legacy of the Victorian era.

When infection is recognized, it needs to be treated, and then further infection needs to be prevented. Treating infection is fairly easy. Preventing further infection can be a real challenge.

The proper approach to treatment is to obtain a urine culture to identify the bacteria and then start the right antibiotic to kill that bacteria. The most common bacteria are E coli, and there are several antibiotics that are good for these bacteria. My preference is nitrofurantoin, an old antibiotic that works well for almost all the types of E coli. If there is obvious infection, I request the parent take in a urine specimen for culture to the lab and then start the antibiotic. When the actual culture result comes back in two to four days, I hardly ever need to change the antibiotic if I've started with nitrofurantoin.

If infection is the only reason that the bladder does not hold enough urine, and therefore the main reason for the bedwetting, then with successful treatment, the wetting should resolve. This happens, but not very often. Usually the infection resolves, but the wetting continues. Even so, treating and preventing infection is still a very important part of the therapy to achieve dryness. Just because the wetting did not resolve does not mean that the infection was not playing an important supportive role in the bedwetting.

If the history does not clarify whether the infection has been smouldering for a long time, I treat the infection for a week or ten days and then check the urine for infection a week later. If the history confirms the infection has smouldered for months or even years, or if the infection promptly returns, this implies considerable inflammation of the bladder wall, and I routinely put these children on three months of preventative antibiotic therapy.

During the three months on continuous preventative antibiotic therapy, the goal will be to improve bladder and bowel health and to improve personal hygiene such that when the preventative antibiotic is stopped, I hope, the infection will not promptly return. If the infection does return right away, I prescribe another three-month course of preventative therapy. I continue to do this until the infection does not return. The initial three-month course is usually all that is necessary.

Many parents do not feel comfortable with three months of daily antibiotic. I wish there was an alternative, but my experience suggests there is not. When infection has smouldered for months and even longer, a single course of antibiotic for seven to ten days is not enough. When the infection comes and goes and promptly returns after the antibiotic is stopped, a three-month course is necessary.

Many parents worry about side effects when their child is taking an antibiotic continuously for months at a time. Side effects can happen with any antibiotic. For nitrofurantoin, the side effect profile is very good. I have used this medication over my entire career, and I have only seen two serious rash reactions and two asthma-like reactions. Tummy pain in the pit of the stomach is a common minor side effect, and this happens in about 10 per cent of children. This usually settles with time or when a child takes something to eat with the medication. Nitrofurantoin turns the urine a dark-orange colour, and this is not a concern; consider this evidence the medication is in the right place to do the job.

Once the antibiotic is stopped, either after a seven-to-ten-day treatment or after a three-month course of preventative therapy, the urine needs to be checked for recurrence of infection. I teach the parents how to check the urine at home. I teach parents to use Multistix, the same tool that a doctor uses to screen for infection during an office visit. Multistix are narrow strips that are dipped into the urine and that test for a variety of different problems and situations. The Multistix that I use test for the presence of sugar, protein, fat, red blood cells, white blood cells, and bacteria. They also test the concentration (specific gravity) and acid-base level (pH). For infection, the only tests that matter are for white blood cells and bacteria. For routine screening, I recommend a first morning urine specimen, but if the child has symptoms, any urine can be tested. The test must be done precisely, and I teach the parent how to do this in the office. If the test is positive, the proper procedure is to obtain a urine culture at a laboratory and start an antibiotic either at once, or when the culture results are available. If there are symptoms of infection, I prefer that the parents start the antibiotic at once, and I make sure they have culture requisitions and a prescription for an antibiotic on hand. If there are no symptoms and only the Multistix test is positive, waiting for the culture report is satisfactory. The next page has a copy of the printed instructions that I give to each parent on how to use the Multistix.

In earlier chapters, I reviewed the principles of good bladder health and bladder-friendly bowel health, but further considerations on these topics are necessary when infection is part of the problem.

Bladder infection is more common in children who do not empty their bladder well. When there are bacteria in the bladder and the bladder doesn't empty, the bacteria are allowed to hang around longer and cause trouble. Emptying completely is a basic defence against bladder infection.

The two most important principles to empty the bladder well are to avoid an overfull bladder and to use great posture to relax the pelvic floor muscles with voiding. This means girls with bladder infection need to void more often just to empty, and they must always respond to the first signal of the need to pee and not hold the urine.

I suggest that children void at common "transition times." A transition time is the time between activities. Peeing when you wake up is the transition from sleep to waking, and peeing at bedtime is the transition from awake to asleep. If a child washes his hands for a meal and he pees before he washes his hands, this is a transition-time pee. Children should "pee before they play." There should be commonsense home rules that before the children play a video game, start a movie on the television, or get absorbed with Lego or Barbies, they should pee. Other common transition times are when the child leaves the house to play in the backyard or leaves the house to get in the car. Peeing at transition times is much easier than asking a child to pee according to an arbitrary schedule. Peeing on a schedule interrupts activities, and most children (or adults for that matter) do not enjoy interrupting their favoured activities.

Squatting is a symptom of an irritable and a pressurized bladder. The squat is a learned response to a sudden bladder contraction. Some girls who have not had infection also learn to squat, but when there is a history of squatting, more often than not, infection has been part of the story. Squatting is more common with infection because an inflamed bladder is less predictable and a sudden bladder contraction catches the girls totally by surprise.

Testing the Urine for Infection with Multistix

For routine tests, when there are no symptoms of infection, always check a first morning urine specimen. Otherwise, check the next urine after symptoms develop.

The first morning urine is the best because this is usually the longest a child goes without voiding and therefore the longest that a germ is around to get established.

Always rinse the genital area well with water for at least a minute before your child voids. A handheld shower nozzle works well. Use a gentle stream and lukewarm water (not too hot, not too cold). Spread the labia and make sure the area between the labia is well rinsed.

Spread the labia, and collect the urine in a glass container (a jam jar will do). Glass is easier to rinse and clean between tests.

Dip the Multistix into the urine and then shake off the excess urine. Place the Multistix on the top of the glass container.

At **precisely sixty seconds** look at the Multistix and compare the colour of the last two squares to the colours on the bottle. If you check the colour after a longer period of time, the result will not be reliable (false-positive test). Always check in a well-lit room.

In the presence of infection, the leukocyte (white blood cell) test square will turn purple. This is the last square on the stick. In the presence of infection, the nitrite (bacteria) test square will turn pink. This is the second-to-last square on the stick.

If the Multistix turns bright purple or pink at sixty seconds, infection is likely. If the Multistix turns an intermediate colour, you should check again after careful rinsing.

If your child has suspicious symptoms and the Multistix suggests infection, you need to take a urine specimen to the lab for routine urinalysis (yellow form) and culture (green form). The specimen needs to be fresh (less than two hours old), the lid needs to be tight, and the bottle must be placed into the special bag. The addresses and opening hours for the labs are on the back of the forms.

The results of a urine culture can take up to four business days to be available. Let Dr. Robson's office know that you have taken a urine specimen to the lab, and they will look for the result.

Always put the top on the Multistix bottle promptly after taking a strip out and avoid leaving the bottle in a humid area (steamy bathroom) because moisture will spoil the Multistix. Note, there is an expiry date on the Multistix.

Girls who squat but who do not have infection as part of the problem are squatting because they routinely tend to postpone voiding but they have decided that a soaker is not acceptable. They accept minor dampness, but they are not prepared to accept a soaker. Sometimes this is a feature of their personality and evolves fairly soon after toilet training, and sometimes this is learned as they get older and daytime wetting becomes socially less acceptable.

The typical squatting posture is for the girl to suddenly sit down on her heel. She pushes the heel between her legs. There is a neural pathway theory that suggests that this posture can stop the bladder contraction, but my sense is that this is just a control posture and that the contraction resolves with time; the squat does not stop the contraction or otherwise reduce this time. The girls learn to do this to prevent a major soaking episode, but they will still be a bit damp.

Preventing a major soaker might sound like a good thing, but I consider squatting to be a red flag that suggests the risk of serious pressure-related bladder damage over time.

The normal sequence of events with peeing is that the sphincter muscle relaxes, urine comes out of the bladder into the urethra, and the presence of the first few drops of urine in the urethra stimulates a nerve reflex that causes the muscles of the bladder wall to contract and push out the urine. Normally, we only allow the external sphincter to relax at an appropriate time, such as when we are sitting on a toilet. However, in girls who hold their urine, who are always saying no to the signal, the pressure can build up to the point when the external sphincter muscle cannot hold in the pee any longer. The bladder is now in a rock-and-a-hard-place position. The rock is the poop wall. The hard place is the sphincter muscle. But something has to give, and the sphincter relaxes and lets off a little pressure. The urine starts to come out, and the girl feels this. The sphincter would actually like to let off all the pressure and allow the bladder to completely empty, but the girl doesn't want that. These girls have learned that soaking causes a lot more displeasure with mothers, fathers, relatives, teachers, and peers than dampness. So the child learns to squat and to contract the sphincter to minimize the wetting.

Recently, during the course of one week, I had two parents who related the terminology that their daughters used to describe what they were trying to accomplish with the squat. The girls used identical terminology. Both told their parents that when they squat they are "sucking [urine] back in."

Squatting at school can be an embarrassment, and as girls get older, they adopt strategies to conceal the squat. These girls might drop something so they can squat while they pick up whatever they dropped. They might pretend to be looking for a contact lens. They might pretend to be getting something out of their pack.

Imagine the pressure in the bladder of these girls! That pressure is not healthy, and girls who squat almost always have a bladder wall that is thicker than average. The cost of avoiding a soaker is high bladder pressure, and over time, this can lead to permanent bladder damage. I would rather the child allowed all the urine to come out! The real solution is to pee more often and never to ignore the signals in the first place.

Girls who squat are often red in the face; they grimace, and sometimes there are tears in their eyes. A squat can last several minutes. Amazingly, some children do not routinely attend the bathroom to pee after a squat. They resume play until the next squat and so on. Ouch!

If a parent tries to carry a child to the bathroom during a squat, the bladder will usually totally empty. Most parents learn not to do this to avoid the mess, but as I said, the pressure-release aspect works for me.

Sometimes a sibling, usually a brother, learns that movement will trigger a major soaker. These brothers, clearly naughty, push their sister over when she squats and then they laugh. Bad boys!

When squatting is part of the history, I stress that an early treatment goal is for the squatting to resolve.

Soiling is a major risk factor for bladder infection. When children let a little bit of poop out in their underwear, this usually guarantees that the bacteria will colonize the genital area.

Soiling happens when the child has been holding the poop in and either some "sneaks" out or they presume they are passing gas and some comes out.

The solution to soiling is a morning poop.

Soiling always happens at an inopportune time.

If the child is at home, she should immediately attend the bathroom to take off the soiled clothes, wipe the area, and rinse the bum and genital area with water. I wish all homes had a bidet, because this is a perfect situation for a bidet rinse.

Lots of children do not immediately attend the bathroom to change and clean. They continue playing. This seems amazing to many parents, but this is common. Some just don't want to interrupt their play. Others do not want to acknowledge the problem because they know the parents will be upset. Some hide the soiled underwear, but you can't hide soiled underwear for long. Dogs find it, and eventually mothers find it.

One mother reported that she found three dozen soiled underwear at the back of the closet in her daughter's room.

I hardly knew what to say.

I had so many questions.

I wondered, *How many pairs of underwear does the child own? How often does the mother do the laundry, or does the mother do the laundry?*

I could not fathom how three dozen pairs of underwear could accumulate without the knowledge of the mother.

The real explanation, I presume, is that both the child and the mother had chosen to hide the problem.

When children hide underwear, I tell the mothers that there needs to be a new set of rules in the house and that pooping in the underwear should never be construed as something that the child will be punished for. Soiling should not turn into "a blame game." The parents must make clear that changing and cleaning after soiling is very important and that the child will never be blamed. In fact, I recommend that parents reward their child for changing and cleaning. If you don't solve the walk-around-with-poop-in-your-underwear problem, you don't solve the bladder-infection problem.

If the soiling happens at school, the child needs to attend the bathroom and do her best to clean up. I would rather she threw out the soiled underwear and returned to class without underwear. Having a change of underwear at school is important if the soiling is common. A child who soils at school, or anywhere outside the home, should have a good water rinse as soon as she returns home.

Routine genital hygiene otherwise includes a rinse every morning after the child takes off the wet pull-up. The chemicals in the pee are enough to cause rashes, especially with a heavy pull-up. I commonly see little red inflamed papules on the bum cheeks, and these can be prevented with morning rinsing. Girls should take care to rinse between the labia with water. The water should be the right temperature for comfort, and no soap is necessary. I recommend a rinse for at least one or two minutes. A bidet would be great, but a handheld shower nozzle works fine.

If the child is red in the genital area, or if the child develops some discomfort with voiding, I recommend a second rinse before bed. If the child has a particularly messy poop, I recommend a rinse after the poop. I don't think you can rinse too often if you are troubled with soiling and bladder infections. Again, I wish every home had a bidet.

After voiding, girls should take care to mop up urine that can be retained behind the labia. When girls sit with their knees together, the urine goes down behind the labia and then into the toilet. Invariably, some of the urine goes down between the bum cheeks to the anus. The chemicals in the urine that is not mopped up and the chronic dampness can lead to redness and irritation. Better posture with the knees apart can minimize this, but the girl should be taught how to mop up the pee between the labia from the front to the back after every void. This is a bigger challenge in girls who are overweight.

After a poop, the girls should be instructed to wipe from front to back.

Bath time presents some risks. Lots of preschool and early elementary children have a good wash, and then they play in the bathtub for long periods of time. The water contains the routine dirt of the day, body soap, and shampoo, and unless the bathtub was cleaned well beforehand, there is also the grime from previous days and previous people. I consider this soupy mix to be a risk factor for infection. If children would like to play in the bath, I recommend that they do the cleaning part, empty the tub, and refill the tub with fresh water for the play portion of the bath. A thorough genital rinse with water is necessary after every bath. Girls need to rinse between the labia, and boys need to gently retract the foreskin and rinse.

Bubble baths have a bad reputation, but so long as girls rinse well after bathing, I do not have a problem with bubble baths.

Bath time is a great time to talk with your child about genital issues. I recommend that parents use this time to discuss genital anatomy, genital hygiene, and how to recognize and avoid sexual predators with preschool and early elementary–aged children, and as appropriate, sexuality, babies, birth control, and sexually transmitted diseases with older elementary–aged children and adolescents.

Summer is often a high-risk time for bladder infection in girls. I review summer bladder infection precautions with the parents. I recommend that girls not spend an entire day in a wet bathing suit. Parents should take several bathing suits on day trips and vacations. After a fun morning of swimming, I recommend a good rinse and a change into underwear and breathable clothes, such as shorts or summer dresses, for an hour or so over lunch. After lunch, I recommend a fresh bathing suit. The child should change into dry clothes for supper.

Swimming in the ocean and rivers with a current is better than swimming in ponds, lakes without much current, and swimming pools. I recommend that parents avoid wading pools that are frequented by infants and toddlers. These pools are very difficult to keep sanitary.

I don't recommend public hot tubs for girls who are prone to bladder infection, or for anyone for that matter. Bacteria are plentiful in hot tubs, and unless the chemicals are perfect, this is a great place to colonize your body with the bacteria from someone else. You probably believe that all the public hot tubs have the chemicals kept in perfect balance. Well, if so, please contact me because have I got a deal for you!

Boys can also develop bladder infection but do so much less often than girls. Good foreskin care is important.

At lot of mothers do not know what to do with a foreskin. Often, a nurse or physician has told these mothers not to touch the foreskin. This is wrong. It is not a question of whether you clean the foreskin, but rather how you clean the foreskin.

I recommend that the penis and foreskin should be rinsed every day with water. The foreskin should be gently retracted until the skin will not go back any further, and then the area should be rinsed with water. No soap is necessary. Once the foreskin does fully retract, a boy or mother should never pull the foreskin back and leave the skin behind the head of the penis. The foreskin should always be promptly pulled forward after cleansing.

Hydration, Hydration, Hydration

Bobby's hydration pattern is typical. He goes to bed thirsty, wakes up, and has only a few ounces of milk with his cereal for breakfast. He drinks very little during the school day. He arrives home thirsty, and in the four or five hours from when he arrives home until bedtime, he drinks the majority of what he drinks during the day.

The graph shows how the kidneys make urine over a typical school day in children who wet the bed. Children who do not wet the bed also make more pee later in the day, but not so excessively. On the bottom of the graph is a typical elementary school day. On the left side of the graph is how much pee the kidneys make every hour during the day.

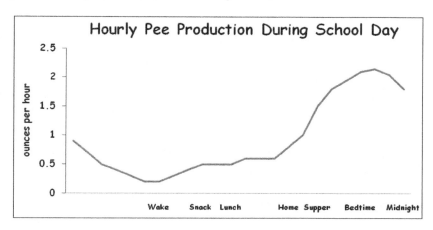

How Bobby drinks during the day fits this graph perfectly. His urine production falls during the last half of the sleep cycle because he went to bed thirsty and did not drink overnight. His urine production stayed low all day at school because the only thing he drank was milk at lunch. He arrived home thirsty and had a glass of juice with his snack, and then he visited the water cooler two or three times before supper. His urine production rate started to increase after that, and the increase continued with the milk and water at supper and with whatever he drank at hockey or from the tap when he brushed his teeth. The rate of urine production was still going up when he went to bed.

His kidneys were happy that he drank all that water later in the day. They were wondering how they were going to process breakfast, morning snack, lunch, and the after-school snack. They did their best with dark, concentrated urine over the day, but they would have preferred more water to work with, and Bobby finally offered that water in the late afternoon and evening.

"Great," said the kidneys, "we can work all night now."

Since Bobby is only eight years old, his bedtime at 8:30 p.m. is only two and half to three hours after supper, which is his biggest meal of the day, and the kidneys will be obliged to process this meal overnight. Bobby sleeps, but his kidneys never sleep.

Bobby loves hockey, and he is either at a practice or a game two or three nights a week, and this includes summer because he goes to hockey camps. He really does want to play in the NHL. On hockey nights, he drinks way more than he needs courtesy of the helpful coach's assistant, and his urine-soaked clothes are proof of that.

Bobby's bladder only holds three ounces. He doesn't have a chance of dryness with this hydration pattern. He has never had a dry night. Go figure!

The hydration rules are fairly straightforward.

Wake up.
Catch up.
Keep up.

Don't come home from school thirsty, and don't go to bed thirsty.

Drink the recommended amount every day, and drink 40 per cent of that amount before lunch. Don't think of milk as a liquid, and always start your day with juice or water.

After sleeping anywhere from a third to almost half of a day, depending on the age of the child, a child needs to replenish his hydration—he needs to catch up—and this should be accomplished with juice or water, not with milk.

Children should have a water bottle at their desk at school, and the parents should specify how much the child should drink before lunch. A good strategy is to put the exact amount the child should drink over the morning in a bottle and tell the child to finish this amount before he eats lunch. Another strategy is to draw a line on the water bottle to indicate where the water level should be at lunchtime. A good rule is that the urine should be a pale colour before lunch. This confirms you have caught up. When the body has enough water for current needs, the urine turns a pale-yellow colour.

Once a child is caught up, he should drink enough to keep up. This means he should drink every time he eats because water will be necessary to process this food and to keep that food soft as it turns into poop. This also means drinking more when he exercises or when the temperature is high.

If your child arrives home from school thirsty, he didn't drink enough during the day.

Think ahead to the evening, and encourage your child to drink enough at supper and for the first hour or so afterwards to make sure he is not thirsty at bedtime.

On sports nights, make sure the child starts the practice or game hydrated and drinks enough during the activity to keep up with sweat loss. If a child doesn't keep up properly with the sweat loss, he will almost always drink more than he needs after the activity, and then he will return home and fall asleep without being able to pee out most of that excess water. This requires practice. You will know you have the right balance when the child is no longer parched and thirsty after the activity. In Bobby's case, he will also come home without having wet his clothes.

Some children sweat profusely, while, for the same energy expenditure, others perspire much less. If your child really sweats a lot, the sweat loss should properly be replaced with a sport drink during the activity. I do not otherwise routinely recommend a sport drink, because the high salt content will definitely increase urine production overnight.

Catching up with hydration in the morning and allowing the kidneys to make more urine during the day reduces the amount of urine the kidneys will make at night.

Catching up with hydration in the morning and keeping up at school prevents after-school and evening thirst. If the child is not thirsty and does not overdrink from the time he gets home from school, the kidneys will produce less urine overnight.

Finally—and this is very important—catching up with hydration in the morning and keeping up throughout the day keeps the poop soft, and soft poop is essential for bladder-friendly bowel health.

As with every child, what Bobby does in the morning affects whether he will wet at night. If he poops in the morning and if he hydrates in the morning, he is on the road to dryness at night.

What children do in the morning determines whether they will wet at night.

Some children arrive at the first visit to my office with bladders that hold less than Bobby's, and some arrive with bladders that hold a lot more.

Generally, those children who arrive at the first visit with a bladder that holds only two or three ounces wet every night and usually multiple times a night. Those children with bladders that hold more might only wet once a night, and some have already had dry nights.

When a child arrives in my office and reports that he is dry on about half the nights, I know that his bladder likely holds more than the children who have never had a dry night. In these children, dryness is sometimes possible by managing hydration alone, without any improvement in how much the bladder can hold and without any improvement in the ability to wake up. This sounds good, but sometimes these children accept improved dryness courtesy of the hydration recommendations, and they do not work on their bowel health. This is a big mistake. Most of these children will continue to wet sporadically because they did not improve their bladder capacity. This is a penny-wise but pound-foolish approach.

By now, you know how to increase how much the bladder will hold and how to reduce how much urine the kidney makes at night. With this approach alone, some children will be dry, especially those who start off with a bladder that holds more from the start. But with this approach, it could take years to achieve dryness in boys like Bobby. These children need to learn how to wake up. Alarm therapy is the tool we use for this, and the next chapter outlines how I treat children with alarm therapy.

Waking Up Is Hard to Do

I am a child of the '60s, and the title of this chapter is adapted from a great song recorded by Neil Sedaka in 1962—"Breaking up is Hard to Do." When I searched the Internet to confirm the year the record was recorded, I learned that several years later, Neil Sedaka actually recorded "Waking up is Hard to Do" as a song for children!

Over the years, I've heard lots of funny stories about how deeply children sleep.

A common comment is, "He sleeps like the dead."

Another is, "A bomb could go off and he wouldn't wake." Several years ago, I had a family from Palestine, and they confirmed that their boy didn't wake up during a time when the Israeli army was shelling their city, so I guess this is true.

Quite a few mothers have told me that if their son falls out of bed, he doesn't wake up.

Several mothers have reported, "I can vacuum in his room, and he doesn't wake."

There are lots of pet stories. "The cat can jump on him and he doesn't wake," or "The dog licks his face and he doesn't wake."

Most parents presume their child will not wake up to a bedwetting alarm, but there are very few children in my clinic who will not wake up if the family follows my instructions.

Most parents have tried waking their child in the middle of the night. Some parents do this when they go to bed. Other parents set alarms at specific times. Some parents do this when they are otherwise up to pee or to care for another child. Almost all the parents report that although their child did manage to pee, the child had absolutely no recollection of this the next morning.

Some parents try waking the child consistently at certain times for a period of weeks or even months. They have been told this will help cure bedwetting, but it doesn't. Since this didn't help, they often presume that alarm therapy will not work either, but it will.

Waking the child up at random times does not help because they are not waking the child up when the bladder is full.

Alarm therapy helps because the alarm goes off after a partial arousal and precisely when the bladder is full and emptying. This makes all the difference.

One mom, who wet the bed as a child, described a variation of alarm therapy that was successful for her. After a move to a new home when she was in elementary school, it became necessary for her to sleep in the same bed as her older sister. The bed was small, and the sister woke promptly every time the warm pee soaked over to her side of the bed. The older sister routinely screamed and punched her in the arm. The wetting resolved. Getting mad the next morning or even fifteen minutes later would not have worked. The scream and punch were an "alarm" that went off immediately after the bladder emptied (warm urine).

Many parents search for a pattern of wetting and expect to find that the wetting will always happen at such and such a time or times, but consistent patterns are not common. They are not common because the hydration and bowel health changes day-to-day—sometimes a little and sometimes a lot—and this will change the time when the bladder will be full.

In a later chapter, we will discuss patterns of dryness and wetting and how to interpret them.

The sequence of sleep events that occur before and after a wetting episode are quiet sleep, partial arousal sleep as the bladder gets closer to full, full bladder, wetting episode, and resumption of quiet sleep. This sequence can play out multiple times, as many times as the bladder fills overnight.

When alarm therapy is started, the sequence of sleep events that occur before and after an episode of wetting are quiet sleep, partial arousal sleep, full bladder, alarm going off at the first drop of urine, child waking up, child going to the bathroom, child returning to bed, and resumption of quiet sleep. On the way to and from the bathroom, the child is presumably thinking about how much of nuisance it is to get up and how much he wishes he were dry. He might think, *That noise was really irritating,* or *I really don't want to get out of my warm bed,* or *Gee, I wish I didn't wet the bed.* The brain hears these thoughts.

Alarm therapy is a conditioning process. The brain needs to be conditioned to change something.

The brain has two opportunities to change something and to improve the situation. The brain could wake the child up during the partial arousal, or the brain could "manage" the bladder and instruct the bladder to hold more and to wait until the child wakes up the following morning. The second option, the "manage the bladder and hold more option," is only possible if the poop that surrounds the bladder is so soft that the bladder can push this poop out of the way.

In the children in my clinic, the brain usually makes both changes during alarm therapy. At the start of alarm therapy, many children learn to wake up during the partial arousal, and later in the conditioning process, they just sleep dry. By the end of alarm therapy, most of the patients in my clinic sleep dry, and they do not need to wake up in the middle of the night to pee.

I do not start alarm therapy in a child until he has improved his bowel health. I won't start prematurely because I want to cure the bedwetting, and the success rate is much higher once the child has achieved bladder-friendly bowel health.

Within the last decade, there was a major review of all the best clinical studies on alarm therapy.[8] The study only reviewed "evidence-based" studies, which implies that the investigating doctors followed the very best possible research standards. The review confirmed that bedwetting could be cured by alarm therapy. When all the studies were analyzed, about two-thirds of the children achieved dryness, but only half of those stayed dry off the alarm. This means that about a third of children become dry and stay dry.

Over the last five years in my practice, over 90 per cent of the patients treated with alarm therapy have achieved dryness and stayed dry.

Why do I get so much better results?

There are probably lots of reasons, but the one that I consider the most important is that I pay attention to bowel health first.

Have I mentioned the importance of the morning poop?

The three factors that are most important for success with alarm therapy are the achievement of bladder-friendly bowel health, a supportive parent, and a motivated or at least compliant child.

Every child will wear the alarm for a minimum of three consecutive months. Consistency is important for any conditioning therapy, and this is certainly the case for alarm therapy.

The two *musts* of alarm therapy are that the child *must* get up with each alarm, pee in the toilet, go back to bed, and put the alarm back on, and a parent *must* get up each and every time with the child. These are absolute musts for success.

---

8   C. M. Glazener, "Alarm Interventions for Nocturnal Enuresis in Children," Cochrane Database of Systematic Reviews, Art. No.: CD002911, doi: 10.1002/14651858, CD002911.pub2 (2005).

I explain to the parent and child that the first two weeks are the toughest. I ask the family to choose a time to start that makes sense for the child, for the parent who will be getting up with the child, and for the family otherwise.

Since the first two weeks are the roughest, I don't recommend that this coincide with the start of the school year or other important events.

Since consistency is important, I recommend that the family choose a time when they are certain they will not be traveling or the home will not otherwise be hectic. Starting alarm therapy within six weeks of major holidays, such as Christmas or Easter, is not a good idea for most families. Summers are usually not a good time for most families. The three traditional best times in my experience are several weeks after the start of the new school year, after the Christmas holidays, and after the spring break. These three times usually offer several months of mostly school routines and less likelihood of travel. Although these are generally good times, any time that offers consistency and otherwise works for the family is a good time.

I book a sequence of appointments when I start children on alarm therapy. I book a coaching session for the day they plan to start, a two-week follow-up, and monthly follow-ups thereafter for three months.

I prefer that one parent be designated to get up with the child, but some parents prefer or are obliged to share this responsibility. If the parents decide to share the responsibility, I insist that both parents attend the coaching session. I've learned that not all parents communicate well with each other. Bet you've never heard that before.

The alarm I recommend is the Malem Ultimate alarm. This alarm is sturdy, has eight different alarm sounds that come on in a random fashion, and vibrates as well. The alarm is small and connects to the underwear of a child with a small clip. I request that the parents purchase the alarm and bring the alarm to the coaching session. I will not start alarm therapy with a lesser quality alarm. The alarms are manufactured in Nottingham, England, and are distributed in North America by The Bedwetting Store, an American company. They cost about US$125.00. Two AAA batteries power the alarm and last for the usual duration of therapy. In the spring of 2010, Malem introduced a wireless alarm with two receivers, one of which can be in the bedroom of the parent. This alarm is US$170.00.

Many health insurance plans will pay for an alarm, and I routinely write letters to help the parents claim the expense.

Lane Robson, MD
FRCP(C), FRCP(Glasgow), FRSPH
111 4411 16th Ave NW
Calgary, Alberta

November 3, 2010

Re: Bobby
DOB: March 26, 2002

Dear Health Insurance Company,

Bobby has voiding problems including bedwetting, and I prescribed a Malem bedwetting alarm to treat this problem. I recommend that the alarm be covered under the health insurance policy for the family.
If you have any questions, please call my office.
Thank you for considering this request.

Very truly yours,

Lane Robson, MD

There are many other alarms available. About twenty years ago, I served on the bedwetting committee for the National Kidney Foundation (NKF). I served on this committee for about ten years, and during these years, our committee included a who's who of doctors in the American bedwetting world. The committee met several times a year, most commonly in New York, which was the headquarters for the NKF. At one meeting, I suggested that we obtain samples of all the commonly available alarms and assess them to decide what makes a good alarm. We obtained eight alarms, and after careful study, the committee came up with a list of the features of an ideal alarm. This list was made available on the NKF bedwetting website to help parents choose an alarm. The list of features included simple design, comfortable to wear, sturdy, and powered by easy-to-obtain batteries. The NKF did not endorse any of the alarms. The Malem Ultimate satisfied all of these features and was the favourite of many members of the committee.

I have a checklist of topics that I review at the coaching session, and afterwards, I give the checklist to the parents to help them remember. This checklist continues to grow as I learn more about how to improve the chances for success. In the future, I will ask parents to purchase a copy of this book.

I am very specific about all my instructions because I want the family to get off to a good start. Beginnings are important, and experience has taught me that you cannot be too specific. I have probably not seen all the mistakes that can be made, but I'm sure I've seen most, and my goal is to minimize frustrations at the start of this therapy.

I review how the alarm works and demonstrate the technical aspects of the alarm.

The clip consists of two metal connections. When clipped onto the underwear, the alarm does not go off, because the fabric between the two metal clips prevents the clips from touching and the electricity from flowing. I use facial tissue as an underwear substitute and clip the tissue. I set the sink faucet in my office on drip and demonstrate that a single drop of water bridges the electrical connection between the two metal connections, which triggers the alarm.

I review how to connect the alarm properly to the underwear and where to pin the alarm on the shoulder of the child.

For children who wear a pull-up, the layered sequence is underwear against the skin, clip on the *outside* of the underwear, and then the pull-up over the underwear.

The clip should be in the middle of the underwear. I recommend cotton underwear. For boys, I prefer briefs that hug rather than loose boxers. The underwear needs to be placed between the entire half inch of the clip connection surface; if just a corner of the connection is clipped, it can be pulled off too easily during sleep, which will cause a false alarm. The alarm should be pinned on top of the shoulder and close to the ear, not on the chest where a pillow could muffle the sound. The connecting wire should go under the pyjamas, nightie, or T-shirt to prevent getting tangled in a restless arm. The wire is always too long and can be bunched up with an elastic band as necessary.

I review how to put the batteries in the device and point out the schematic inside the compartment, because how the batteries are inserted is not intuitive to everyone.

There is a switch inside the battery compartment, and this switch can be set to alarm only, vibrate only, or to alarm and vibrate. The switch should always be on both the alarm and vibrate setting, which is the middle setting in the alarm. I tell the parents never to set the switch only on vibrate. The noise is essential.

I demonstrate the eight different noises and point out that two of the noises take slightly longer to turn off, because this confuses some parents.

I discuss how to clean the alarm. Pee has chemicals and can be sticky when it dries. Mothers understand this because they are usually the ones who clean up the sticky yellow drips on the toilet seat, toilet rim, and floor—and sometimes the walls, too. The alarm should be rinsed in water and dried thoroughly with tissue. I recommend a rinse in the morning, so there is enough time for the alarm to thoroughly dry over the course of the day.

Some children play with the alarm during the day. They take the batteries out and put them back in. They click the connector in and out of the alarm. They flick the connecting clip back and forth. The alarm is sturdy enough for most situations, but the connection and the clip can break and become loose. For most children, the alarm is best stored in the bedroom of the parent.

After reviewing these technical details, I outline the rules.

The child must get up with each alarm, go to the toilet and finish peeing, change into dry underwear, return to bed, and always reattach the alarm. The child must do this every time the alarm goes off, no matter how many alarms occur during the night and no matter whether the last alarm is within an hour of the usual wake-up time. If the child goes back to bed, he should put the alarm back on.

The responsible parent must get up with each alarm and supervise this process.

Before the alarm can be turned off, *the child must be sitting up in the bed with the legs over the side of the bed; the parent must be present in the child's room; and the adult must be convinced that the child is awake.* If the child can make eye contact and can carry on a coherent conversation, the child is likely awake.

The child must be able to remember the alarm the next morning. If the child does not remember the alarm, he was not fully awake. The next morning, the parent should ask the child, "Did the alarm go off?" She should not ask if the child remembered getting up, because some children will say yes even if they do not remember. The parent needs to phrase the question such that the child can offer an unbiased answer. If the child does not remember, the parent needs to adopt further strategies. A moist, cool cloth on the face, walking around with the child, or asking the child questions are common strategies that help to ensure the child is really awake.

Recently, a dad, who was a psychologist, made a good suggestion. He suggested that parents show the child a picture of something, such as a number or a fruit and then ask the child the next morning to describe the picture.

Some of the younger or less mature children are frightened by the alarm.

They wake up crying. This is not common, but I mention this to every child regardless of age because this can even happen in an adolescent. I discuss how the child can mentally prepare for this possibility. I ask the child to tell his mother before bed, "Mom, I will not be frightened if the alarm goes off." A frightened and crying child can understandably distress parents, but I recommend that they carry on because the crying is less with each successive night. If the child does wake up crying, this usually happens only on the first night. Occasionally, this can recur on the second or third night. I have only had one child go more than three nights. This child cried every night for the first week. I have had only one alarm failure because a child cried with the alarm. These parents stopped after the first few nights.

Some children scream and fight when the mother tries to wake them. These children will punch, slap, and use words that the mother did not realize were part of her child's vocabulary. I discuss this with every family, and I discuss how the child can mentally prepare for this possibility. I ask the child to tell his mother before bed, "Mom, I will not try to fight if you try to wake me up." This also happens less and less each night, and I recommend that parents carry on. I have never had an alarm failure because the child continued fighting.

The child is not allowed to turn the alarm off. This is a very bad practice. The child will easily learn to turn the alarm off and fall right back asleep. The parent should always be the one to turn the alarm off.

Initially, the parent might need to help the child to wake up. The parent might need to speak to the child, move the child, gently shake the child, help the child to sit up, stand the child up, and such and so forth, to help the child wake up. However long this takes the first night, the length of time usually gets less each night. A common amount of time on the first night is about five minutes. The longest a parent has every reported is about fifteen minutes. *No matter how long the child takes to wake up, the parents must resist the temptation to turn off the alarm before the child is awake and can actually hear the alarm.* Most parents presume they will need to help their child to wake up, but my experience is that more than half of the children are awake and waiting for the parent to arrive from the very first night.

Most parents worry that the alarm will wake up and disturb the sleep of other family members, but after the first week, this is uncommon. Even siblings who sleep in the same room seem to be able to disregard the noise after the first week. The exceptions might be a newborn infant, but many of these babies sleep through as well. Elderly grandparents with insomnia can be a concern, and earplugs might help in this situation. Close the doors to the rooms of other family members.

The mother must be able to hear the alarm, because she must get up each and every time the alarm goes off. Most mothers presume they will wake up. Common comments are, "I can hear every time my son rolls over in his bed," or "I can hear a pin drop in the house at night." About a quarter of mothers who are certain they will wake up don't hear the alarm and don't wake up. If the mother cannot hear the alarm, she must set up a baby monitor in the room or she must change the sleeping arrangements such that either the mother sleeps in the child's room or the child sleeps in the parents' room. The new wireless Malem alarm with a second receiver for the parents' room is also a solution.

If parents decide to share the responsibility to get up, they need to set up a schedule. Without a schedule, one parent nudges the other, the other nudges back, and after a few nudges, they both fall back asleep.

This is a classic case of nudge, nudge, forty winks. Groan! I just now thought that one up.

Even if the child is difficult to wake up, this will improve with practice, and the parents must ensure that the child is awake before the alarm is turned off. Even if the parent takes five or ten minutes to wake the child, which is unusual, the parent is not allowed to turn off the alarm until he is sitting up with the legs over the side of the bed and definitely awake. In really difficult-to-wake children—and this is a small group—the first two weeks can be spent just getting the child to the point where he can wake on his own. Most accomplish this in the first week.

The parent should turn the alarm off. Turning the alarm off requires two procedures in the correct sequence. First, the alarm must be unclipped from the underwear. The child may do this. Second, the button on the side of the alarm must be pressed. This button is stiff and requires substantial pressure. This is usually best accomplished with a pinching manoeuvre by placing a finger or thumb over the button and another finger on the other side of the alarm.

There are two places where the alarm can be disconnected. The alarm can be disconnected from the clip on the underwear, and the alarm can be disconnected from the alarm, per se. The connecting wire enters the alarm with the same kind of connection as a home phone. The child should only disconnect the alarm where the clip connects to the underwear. This needs to be done because the child needs to walk to the bathroom. The child should not disconnect the alarm at the phone clip (alarm) end. This is too easy and might encourage the child to do it lying down, which is a bad practice because many children learn to turn the alarm off quickly and just fall back asleep. Another reason for the child not to disconnect the phone clip end is that this end is easier to break. The tiny plastic lever that is pressed to release the connection can break off.

Practicing before you start makes a difference. In the middle of the night, the alarm sounds very loud against the background of stillness and silence. Some parents are certain that the entire neighbourhood can hear the noise. Some parents and children have a sense of urgency to stop the noise. Practice makes this easier to accomplish.

The worst story I've heard of how a parent dealt with this sense of urgency to stop the noise was of the parent who finally threw the alarm on the floor and stomped on the device until the noise stopped.

This sort of frustration can be avoided by following the rule that you disconnect first and push the button second, and by practicing this sequence while totally awake, before the child wears the alarm on that first night.

Once the child can wake up on his own, he needs to practice waking up so fast that he limits the amount of pee to only a small stain in the underwear. I tell the child that this is his responsibility, that this is something that only he can do, that his parents cannot do this for him. I tell him he needs to "wake up faster and stop peeing sooner." This is the most important responsibility of the child, and I repeat this at least five times during the coaching session. I ask the child to talk or think about this every time he puts on the alarm. He should say to his parent or to himself, "I'm going to wake up faster tonight, and I'm going to have less pee (only a drop) in my pull-up (sheets, underwear) and more pee in the toilet."

The first night, the amount of urine in the pull-up is usually a large amount, and the amount of urine left to pee in the toilet is small. The child needs to learn to wake up faster and faster and to stop peeing sooner and sooner, such that there are only a few drips in the underwear and more and more pee in the toilet. I ask the parents to keep track of this on a special calendar. The time the alarm goes off is recorded. The amount of pee in the pull-up is scored 3 if the pull-up is heavy, 2 if there is an average amount in the pull-up, and 1 if the urine is limited to the underwear and not in the pull-up at all. The amount the child pees in the toilet can be measured with an inexpensive urine collection container that fits in the rim of the toilet. These are available at medical supply outlets and at some pharmacies. The child is asked to practice getting up sooner and sooner until the wetting amount is always a 1.

I tell parents that a reasonable outcome for the first two weeks is for the child to wake on his own, for the child to wake easier and sooner, and for the mother and the child to become a team. Many mothers are up with their child for about fifteen minutes on the first night. The amount of time that they are up should get progressively less, such that by the two-week follow-up appointment, most mothers and the child are back in bed in less than five minutes.

A successful pattern is for the alarm to initially go off multiple times a night and then only once, and then for the child to start to have dry nights.

Another successful pattern is for the alarm to go off progressively later in the sleep cycle. The alarm might go off at midnight the first night, 1:00 a.m. the second night, 2:00 a.m. the third night, and so on as alarm therapy continues. This pattern implies that the brain is "managing" the bladder and instructing the bladder to hold more urine. Remember, this only happens when the bladder is surrounded by soft, mushy poop.

If the child wakes up in the middle of the night to pee without the alarm going off, this is a successful pattern. This implies that the child is waking up during the partial arousal, and this confirms that the ability of the child to arouse has improved. I make sure that the child understands that if he does wake up in the middle of the night, he might not feel like he needs to pee, but he must pee. He must also tell his mother so she can record the time and the voided volume. The child and mother should celebrate when a child wakes up to pee. A "high five" is in order or a "happy dance," because this is a highly desired outcome. The brain needs a strong emotional signal to consolidate this behaviour. Waking to pee is the best defence against bedwetting, because everyone occasionally drinks too much in the evening and exceeds his bladder capacity.

Of course, the ultimate successful pattern is more and more dry nights.

At some point within the first few weeks or month, about half the children will wake up wet and no one heard an alarm. Most parents presume this is a technical problem, but 90 per cent of the time, what has happened is that the child woke up, turned the alarm off very quickly while lying down, and promptly fell back asleep. The children learn to turn the alarm off in seconds. If this happens, the sleeping arrangements need to be changed and either the child must sleep in the parents' room or the mother must sleep in the child's room. If the mother does not hear the alarm and therefore does not ensure that the child wakes up to void, then conditioning will not happen and alarm therapy will be unsuccessful. The new wireless Malem alarm is a solution to this problem.

In this situation, most of the children deny that they turned off the alarm. To admit this would confirm that they broke one of the fundamental rules of alarm therapy. Some of the children legitimately do not remember turning off the alarm, but others do. Whether the child is telling the truth or not does not make any difference. The important point is to recognize that the sleeping arrangements need to be changed and that the mother must hear the alarm and ensure compliance with the rules.

There are a few technical reasons why a child might wet and the alarm did not go off. If the phone clip is not "clicked" into place or if the underwear clip is not fastened on the underwear, then the alarm will not go off. If the underwear clip is not positioned such that the urine will reach the sensor, the alarm will not go off. Good technique prevents these possibilities.

The alarm is an obnoxious noise. Most children do not enjoy waking up to the alarm. Some children really don't like the alarm, and they resort to a variety of methods to prevent the alarm from going off. Once the parents leave the room, some children unclip the alarm. Others put the batteries in backwards. There will not be an alarm in these situations. Parents usually presume there is a technical problem. I tell the parents at the outset to look for these ruses.

An unsuccessful pattern at the two-week follow-up is indicated if the child never woke up without the help of the parent or if the parent continues to take a long time to wake the child up. This is not a hopeful pattern, and this is uncommon.

At the two-week follow-up, I troubleshoot technical problems and correct misconceptions. I make sure the mother and child are a team.

The most important part of this appointment is to reinforce the importance of waking up sooner and sooner. I stress that consistency is very important, and I tell the child he is not allowed to get lazy. I am always looking to point out the positive and to reinforce the successes. However, if the child presents as not fully compliant, I am blunt about the potential outcome if he doesn't improve. He needs to keep on task.

I ask the children to celebrate the nights when they wake up so fast that there is only a small amount of pee in their underwear. They could say out loud and with conviction, "I'm number one!"

I also suggest that they get a bit upset with themselves if they wake up slower and soak into the pull-up or sheets. They need to feel real disappointment. Strong emotions are good for conditioning.

At the two-week follow-up, I am usually able to predict whether alarm therapy will be successful and how long that alarm therapy will be necessary.

I ask the children to wear the alarm every night for a minimum of three consecutive months. If the noise of the alarm would be indiscreet in a special circumstance, such as if a relative sleeps over in the home or if the family is away over a weekend and is staying with family or friends, I recommend that the child wear the alarm but not connect the clip to the underwear. Putting the alarm on each night and taking the alarm off each morning is part of the conditioning process. This confirms that the child is thinking about the project. While the child is asleep, the brain is certainly aware that the alarm is on the shoulder of the child.

About half the children will only need to wear the alarm the basic three months. Another quarter will wear the alarm for one further month, and the final quarter will wear the alarm for a longer period. So long as the child shows month-by-month improvement, I continue therapy.

My criteria to stop alarm therapy are:

- the child is dry at least 90 per cent of nights (no more than three alarms in the last month);
- on the infrequent occasions when the alarm does go off, the child wakes up so promptly that there is only a small stain in the underwear;
- the child is no longer in pull-ups, and
- the child is not thirsty at bedtime and can purposefully drink at least four ounces of water or juice an hour before bedtime and still be dry more than 90 per cent of nights.

I ask the child to stop wearing the pull-up as soon as he demonstrates the ability to wake up so promptly that there is consistently only a small stain in the underwear and nothing in the pull-up. This is an important achievement for the child. The night they stop wearing a pull-up is a big night. When a child is able to stop wearing the pull-up, the end is in sight!

Some children are reluctant to stop wearing the pull-up. They need to be reminded that they can wake up so quickly that the urine is limited to their underwear. The mom needs to reassure them that even if some pee ends up in the sheets, this will be okay.

Stopping the pull-ups is like taking the training wheels off a two-wheeler.

Once the child achieves dryness in the 90 per cent range, I ask him to purposefully drink four ounces of water or juice every night, about an hour before bedtime. An important goal is dryness without bedtime thirst or overnight dehydration.

Failure of alarm therapy is not common in the children treated in my clinic, but this does happen in about 10 per cent of the cases. If the child cannot wake to the alarm without the help of the parents at the two-week follow-up, if there are still multiple alarms every night, and if the mother and child are sleep deprived, I consider this failure, and I stop alarm therapy. If the child does not show month-to-month improvement over two consecutive months, I consider this a failure and stop alarm therapy.

One of the reasons why I have so much success with alarm therapy is because once the child has achieved bladder-friendly bowel health, the risk of multiple alarms every night and the number of nights that multiple alarms will persist is minimized. When the bowel health is not improved first, the bladder is surrounded by pasty, hard poop and cannot hold very much. The alarm will go off multiple times and will continue to go off multiple times, and there are few parents or children who can handle this much sleep deprivation for more than a few weeks. The parents and children wear out.

I do not treat sleep deprivation lightly. A sleep-deprived child or parent will not be focused at school or at work. Sleep-deprived children and adults are prone to accidents. If alarm therapy is not progressing well and I sense either the parent or the child is wearing out, I consider this a good reason to stop alarm therapy. Sometimes the parent or child wants to continue, but if the child is falling asleep in class and if the mother arrives looking more tired than usual, I am reluctant to continue.

When people are tired, they are often irritable, and arguments that would not otherwise occur are more common. When parents or a parent and child return for the two-week follow-up and they are quick to argue, this usually means they are not getting enough sleep, and this is not a good sign.

If You Can't Count It, It Doesn't Count

If someone keeps track of a behaviour that he or she would like to change, the keeping track itself leads to improvement. This is why some people who would like to lose weight keep a calendar of their daily weight or of their daily calorie counts. The calendar is a reminder that this is an important project for the person. The calendar shows whether progress happens or not and helps the person to adjust his or her routines. The calendar keeps the person on track to success.

From the first visit to my office, I ask the parents to keep a daily calendar of poop and pee. The families that keep a calendar do better than those that don't. When the families who do not improve return for follow-up, they almost invariably do not bring in a calendar. Many of them "forgot" the calendar, or there was some other "good" reason why they do not have information to show me.

The most common reasons are that the calendar "was left on the kitchen table" or "lost somewhere." Others include that the calendar "had coffee poured all over it," "is in the other car," or "was eaten by the dog." There are a handful of people in my practice with dogs that favour pee and poop calendars. Go figure.

Some people keep a perfect calendar, and that is great. Attentive people usually progress faster.

Some people try to fool me and write all the entries at once, likely the evening before the next appointment. In these calendars, every entry is written in the same handwriting, the same ink, and in neat columns. I must really look stupid to some people.

Most people keep a calendar that shows they are paying attention more often than not, and this is fine. I don't expect the calendar to become a central focus in the day-to-day life of a family.

The calendar I recommend is satisfactory for the majority of families. Occasionally, a family decides to design a new calendar that makes better sense to them. I love this. These families almost always do great.

Some parents expect their child to keep the calendar. This is unrealistic for the majority of children, and I do not encourage this unless the child is above-average motivated and clearly capable of the task. My sense is that this might be a reasonable task for some adolescents, but even many of these children benefit from a parent's assistance with record keeping. Working on dryness requires a team approach, with responsibilities for both the parent and the child. The parent should provide the structure, encourage the child, and keep the calendar. If the parent and child fill the calendar out together, this confirms that they are both working on the project.

I recommend that the parent and child discuss the data on the calendar for a few minutes every day. Bedtime is often a convenient time for this discussion.

Most parents view the calendars as a record-the-data-project that I have assigned. They present the completed document to me in the same fashion that a student might hand in some memory homework that did not require any thought.

I prefer the parents to view the record as a tool. Most keep a good record but never look at the results. I would like families to look for patterns. Most don't look for patterns or otherwise study the chart. In any event, my job is to explain the results to the family. With each follow-up visit, I point out the patterns. I help the child to learn about his bowel health, his bladder health, and his hydration.

The basic calendar is a daily record for four weeks. On the left side of the calendar is the day of the week, and in the next column is the date. The weekends are highlighted a different colour. Weekends are always different for both poop and pee, and studying the differences helps a child and family to understand how the body works.

When the family returns for follow-up and an early elementary–aged child hands me the calendar, I sometimes respond with a rhyme.

"Thank you." I smile.
A full report from you,
about your pee and pooh,
or
A full report for me,
about your poop and pee.

The children only hear the toilet words, and they recognize the rhyme. They almost always smile back.

Basic Poop and Pee Calendar

Bobby	Date	1st Poop Time	Hard H Paste P Mush M	2nd Poop Time	Hard H Paste P Mush M	Bedtime Pee Volume	Wet W Dry D	First A.M. Volume
Mon	Nov 8							
Tue	9							
Wed	10							
Thu	11							
Fri	12							
Sat	13							
Sun	14							
Mon	15							
Tue	16							
Wed	17							
Thu	18							
Fri	19							
Sat	20							
Sun	21							

Poop Calendars

There are columns to write down the times for two poops every day. Most children don't even poop once a day at the start, so the second column is to remind them that this is a later goal.

The families are instructed to write down the time of the poop. The patterns are almost always random at the start. Our goal is a morning poop before the child leaves for school.

Have I told you how important it is to poop in the morning?

There is a second set of columns to write down what the poop looks like. The parent can score the poop H for hard, P for paste, or M for mush. Almost all poop is hard or pasty at the start. Our goal is mush, but not in the first few weeks, perhaps by the end of the first month.

If a child already has problems with soiling, I add a column for the family to write down when an episode of soiling occurred. Soilings are almost always later on a day when there was no morning poop. The solution to soiling is a morning poop. The goal is less and less and finally no soiling.

Basic Poop Calendar

Bobby	Date	1st Poop Time	Hard H Paste P Mush M	2nd Poop Time	Hard H Paste P Mush M	Soil Time
Mon	Nov 8					
Tue	9					
Wed	10					
Thu	11					
Fri	12					
Sat	13					
Sun	14					

With the poop record, the family should look back at the end of every week and determine if there has been progress. Did the child poop on more days this week compared to last week? Were there more first morning poops this week compared to last week? Was there less soiling this week? If there was no progress, the parent and child should decide what to change so that they will improve the subsequent week. Did the child really sit every morning? Was the family too rushed for him to sit in the morning? What can the family change to minimize the rush? Did the parent remember to give the poop softener every day and with every meal? Did the parent remember to mix the poop softener in the juice or water that was sent with lunch? Are the hydration goals improving? Every week the family should look for ways to improve. When the family uses the calendar as a tool to change behaviours, progress is a lot faster.

Offering a reward works for some children, especially younger, less mature, and less well-motivated children. Progress is possible when a child is compliant with the recommendations, and rewards can improve compliance.

Ideally, the reward should be the personal satisfaction of a job well done, and at the end of the project, when the child is dry, a child always has this important sense of satisfaction. However, along the way—and the way can be long for many families—incentives can make a difference to sustain interest and compliance.

Rewards should be offered for compliance with a behaviour that will lead to success rather than with the end result.

I would reward sitting for ten minutes every morning rather than the child having a morning poop. I would reward the consistent achievement of a morning hydration target at school.

So now you know how to keep a log of the poops. Groan, another poopy pun. Seriously, this isn't hard. Double groan.

Pee Calendars

The basic pee calendar records whether the child is W for wet in the morning or D for dry.

I ask the parent to purchase an inexpensive urine collection container. These plastic containers fit inside the rim of the toilet and the amount of pee can be easily measured in ounces or millilitres.

Sometimes these containers are called "pee hats" because they look like a hat if you turn them upside down, especially like the hats worn by nuns.

Parents should measure the volume of pee voided at three specific times. The amount should be measured when the child pees at bedtime. Presuming the parent goes to bed later than the child—and this is the case for most parents until the child is close to adolescence—I ask the parent to take the child to the bathroom when he goes to bed. The third specific time I ask the parent to measure the volume of pee is when the child wakes up in the morning. The child should always pee *as soon as he gets up*, and this volume should be recorded.

Basic Pee Calendar

Bobby	Date	Bedtime Pee Volume	Parent Take Time	Parent Take Volume	Wet W Dry D	First A.M. Volume
Mon	Nov 8					
Tue	9					
Wed	10					
Thu	11					
Fri	12					
Sat	13					
Sun	14					
Mon	Nov 15					
Tue	16					
Wed	17					
Thu	18					
Fri	19					
Sat	20					
Sun	21					
Mon	Nov 22					
Tue	23					
Wed	24					
Thu	25					
Fri	26					
Sat	27					
Sun	28					

Always Pee at Bedtime

At least 10 per cent of the children I see for the first time do not pee at bedtime. Since the child has come to my clinic because he wets the bed, this is an amazing statement. The two main reasons why these children don't pee at bedtime are that they don't feel full at bedtime, and they have "accepted" their wetness.

Remember the graph that showed the "evening surge" in pee production in children who wet the bed? Peeing right at bedtime is very important so that as much of that "evening surge" as possible is emptied.

Many children will only pee if they feel full, and if they do not feel full, they presume they do not need to pee. Since many of the children I see have a blurry definition of full, this is not a good strategy. The best strategy is to pee immediately before you climb into bed. Some children read in bed at night, and some are up reading for thirty to sixty minutes. The last thing these children should do before turning out the light is pee one last time. I recommend that the child have both the ceiling light and the reading light on. Since he is obliged to get up to turn off the ceiling light, he might as well nip into the bathroom and pee.

Parents should not presume that just because the child is in the bathroom that the child will pee. Some children go into the bathroom at the request of the parent, don't pee, and then flush the toilet to give the illusion of voiding. This happens! These children don't get that they need to pee even if they don't feel full. Every ounce that is emptied counts towards dryness.

Some children wet the bed every night and have never had a dry night. They do not presume they will have a dry night, and they do not bother to pee at bedtime because they know they will wet regardless of whether they pee at bedtime or not. These children use the same argument for drinking at bedtime. They know they will be wet whether they drink or not, so why not drink? These children have accepted wetting as their "default" situation. Many of these children routinely soak through the pull-up into the bedsheets. Peeing at bedtime would at least minimize the laundry.

Take Your Child to Pee
When You Go to Bed

Notice that this specifies that the parent *take* the child, not wake the child. This is because I don't want to interfere with the sleep of the child any more than necessary. The vast majority of children would have considerable difficulty waking up anyway. The British doctors call this intervention "lifting," because they presume the parent will carry the child to the bathroom. This works for preschool children, but lifting becomes an increasing challenge as the child grows through elementary school. For children who cannot be carried, I ask the parents to direct the sleeping child to the bathroom and sit them on the toilet. Boys should sit too. As soon as the warm bum touches the cold seat, most children will pee. Their sleeping body remembers this sensation and automatically relaxes the external sphincter. Parents should not presume the child is awake enough to walk safely and should always escort the child back to bed.

A normal bladder that is not overfull will completely empty once voiding starts. When a parent takes a child to pee, the bladder is not overfull, so as soon as the pee starts, the bladder will completely empty. As long as there is an ounce of urine in the bladder, a child will empty. Except in the chronically dehydrated child, there is almost always more than an ounce at this time.

Taking the child to pee is not a cure for bedwetting. This is only an intervention that allows us to learn about the evening surge in pee production, which might also result in dry nights. However, the goal is dryness without the need for parental intervention, and eventually the parent will stop this intervention.

There are three goals with this intervention. One is to measure the amount of pee several hours after the child falls asleep.

Presuming that the child peed at bedtime, the amount of pee two hours later will reflect the urine production rate during this time. For parents interested in math, this is an interesting number to study, and it can be very helpful to learn how to manage hydration properly.

The kidneys are continuously making urine. So long as there is an adequate blood pressure, the kidneys will make pee every second of every minute of every hour of the entire day. How much pee the kidneys make at any given moment depends on the hydration status of the child. An average of an ounce an hour is a reasonable amount for the kidney to make overnight. A six-year-old sleeps for ten and a half hours, and the average bladder capacity at this age is 275 millilitres or about 9 ounces. This means that for a six-year-old who doesn't wet the bed, the kidney can make an average of 1.1 ounces per hour. For a ten-year-old who sleeps for nine hours a night and who has an average bladder capacity of 335 millilitres or about 11 ounces, the number is 0.8 ounce per hour. So, an ounce an hour is a reasonable amount to expect the bladder to handle overnight. Now, this is an average, and invariably, the kidney makes pee faster in the first few hours of the night (evening surge), because of the way these children eat and drink. So, for the average to work out to be an ounce an hour over the entire night, the rate in the first few hours can be higher because the rate in the last few hours will be lower.

For parents interested in math, you are probably a few steps ahead of me now, but for those who would like to have something to think about, please keep reading.

Let's go back to Bobby and look at the numbers that his mom brought to me at the first follow-up visit. Mom makes sure Bobby pees at bedtime at 8:30 p.m. He usually falls asleep within ten or fifteen minutes. Before Mom went to bed at 10:30 p.m., she took Bobby to pee and recorded the volume. Bobby always peed. The amount of urine that was made over the two hours between bedtime and when Mom took him to pee varied from one ounce to four ounces. He was already wet about half the nights, and in this case, he usually peed only one or two ounces, but several times, he was already wet and peed three or four ounces. When he was dry, he always peed three or four ounces.

Recollect that we determined that Bobby's daytime bladder was full at about 90 millilitres or 3 ounces. This fits well with seeing a maximum volume of 4 ounces. The bladder can usually hold a bit more at night than during the day. The reasons for this are because there is no pressure from the standing and walking body on top of the bladder and because we are asleep and not emotionally active. Later in the sleep cycle, another reason is because the bladder fills slowly, and a more slowly filling bladder will hold more. Early in the sleep cycle, this is not usually the case.

If Bobby was wet, he likely emptied at about three ounces, and if we add the amount he peed two hours later, we will estimate how much pee he made in two hours. If we divide this by two, we will estimate how much pee he made per hour. We could weigh the pull-up and accurately determine the amount he actually peed, but I don't suggest this to parents. Some parents who are scientists and math people do this on their own, and that is fine by me.

When Bobby was wet, he usually peed only 1 or 2 ounces, and if we add 3 ounces, this means 4 to 5 ounces, and if we divide this by 2, we get 2 to 2.5 ounces per hour. However, a few times, he peed 3 or 4 ounces, and if we add 3, this means 6 to 7 ounces. When we divide this by 2, we get 3 to 3.5 ounces per hour. When Bobby was dry, he consistently peed 3 or 4 ounces, and if we divide this by 2, we get 1.5 to 2 ounces per hour.

Doing the math tells us that he is dry when his mother takes him on nights when he makes 1.5 to 2 ounces per hour, and he is wet on nights when he makes 2 to 4 ounces per hour. This makes perfect sense.

When I looked at the calendar, I asked Mom to identify hockey nights. He was consistently wet on hockey nights and also on Friday and Saturday (weekend) nights. He was usually dry on non-hockey nights. Like most boys, he drinks too much in the evening on hockey nights and on weekend nights, and this increases his pee production rate.

The pee-production rate in the early evening defines the slope of the pee curve. When the rate is high and the slope is steep, dryness is impossible. When the rate is lower and the slope is not as steep, dryness might be possible, depending on how much the bladder can hold.

From a practical perspective, I ask the parent to take the child to pee at the latest time that the parent is still up and when the child will still be dry. This requires some trial-and-error work to find the correct time.

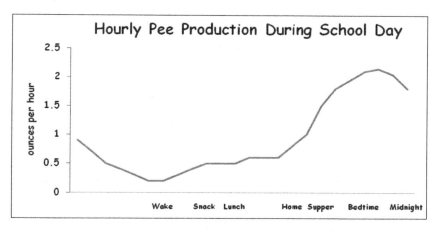

125

Recollect that we would like to see an average of about one ounce an hour overnight to achieve dryness, if we have a normal-sized bladder. Precious few of the elementary-aged children who come to my office have an average-sized bladder. Once parents start to look at these numbers and realize that their child's bladder holds so much less, they start to appreciate the major role that bladder capacity plays in the bedwetting. I hope this convinces them that working on bowel health is very important.

I think by now I must have told you how important it is to poop every morning.

How can Bobby use this information? The parents should do the calculation every night and should compare the number to the prior day. They should think about Bobby's hydration over the day. I teach that anything more than two ounces an hour is too high; anything lower than one ounce per hour is too low, and between one and two ounces an hour is okay.

The kidneys don't lie.

The kidneys don't lie; kidneys make the correct decision about whether our body needs water (if it does, the kidneys hold on to water) or whether our body has too much water (if it does, the kidneys get rid of water). Generally, when the number is high, this means the child had more to drink than was necessary for good hydration and the kidney made a good decision to get rid of excess water. When the number is low, this means the child did not have enough for good hydration, and the kidney made a good decision to hold on to water. While this might result in dry nights, this is not the correct way to achieve dryness.

I do not recommend that parents radically change routines to achieve dryness. I want the boys to play hockey, and I want the boys to have fun on weekend evenings. But I would like them to be practical about how much they drink with hockey and sensible about how much they drink on weekend evenings. This number is a tool the parent can use to insert some common sense into the activity. If Bobby plays hockey and every night his number is high, he needs to practice drinking a little less with each practice until the number falls. Not every parent is up for this kind of fine-tuning, but this is how I crunch the numbers when the parents bring back the calendars.

What Bobby eats in the evening also has an impact on the amount of urine that will be produced overnight. Children who eat late dinners, who graze from supper to bedtime, and who eat salty snacks in the evening and children who always have a bedtime snack will all make more pee overnight than those who eat at the conventional 5:00 to 6:00 p.m. dinner hour, who don't graze, who don't choose salty snacks, and who don't have a bedtime snack. Sometimes their eating behaviours can be changed, and sometimes they can't. I recommend that children enjoy their dinner at a reasonable hour, don't graze or eat salty snacks, and limit bedtime snacks to those nights when the calories are actually necessary.

I mentioned there were three reasons to take the child to pee when the mother goes to bed. The second reason is that if the mother can figure out the right time when the child is still consistently dry, and depending on how much the bladder can hold, this intervention might result in some dry nights.

Now, dry nights are dry nights, and although this intervention has no cure potential, a dry night is always a good thing. Sometimes dry nights can be an important motivator to sustain interest and compliance. Sometimes the intervention is not enough to achieve a dry pull-up but enough to prevent wetting in the sheets. Most mothers are very happy to do less laundry. Eventually, I stop this intervention, usually at the start of alarm therapy.

The third reason to take the child to pee when the mother goes to bed is because this might shift the timing of the full bladder to later in the sleep cycle at a time when the child might be able to wake up to the signal of a full bladder and pee on his own. I tell the child that if he finds himself awake in the middle of the night, he needs to get up and pee, even if he doesn't feel as if his bladder is full. He should tell his mother that he woke up so she can record the time and the volume of urine peed and also so that they can celebrate this highly desired outcome.

Measuring the First Morning Pee Volume

There is almost always pee in the bladder when the child wakes up, regardless of how wet the pull-up or the sheets were. Unless the last void was within the last hour or two of waking up, there will be at least an ounce. Children can empty their bladder as long as there is about an ounce of urine.

The first morning void can tell us useful information.

If a child already has some dry nights, the largest amount peed first thing on a dry morning is a good estimate of how much the bladder can hold at night. This number is always larger than the amount the bladder can hold by day, but sometimes not by much. As mentioned earlier, the bladder can hold more at night because the weight of the upright standing, walking, or running body is not on top of the bladder. Also, after the evening surge is over, the bladder fills more slowly overnight, and a bladder that fills more slowly can hold more. A final reason for a larger night bladder could be the absence of the excitement of the day. Most children will pee at a smaller volume when they are excited. At night, dreams excluded, there is a lot less excitement.

As the bowel health improves and the bladder capacity increases, the largest amount peed first thing in the morning will slowly—emphasis on slowly—increase.

If a child has wet during the night, the largest amount peed first thing in the morning serves as a minimum estimate of how much the bladder can hold at night.

If a child has wet during the night and the first morning volumes are consistently only one or two ounces, this implies that the child likely wet within the last few hours before he woke up. This is a positive pattern because this implies that his bladder almost held enough for him to be dry in the morning. Small numbers on a wet morning suggest the child is close to dryness.

If the mother takes him to pee overnight and he is dry at that time and also in the morning, the sum of the two voids is exactly the amount of urine that the kidneys made overnight. This can help us understand how we are doing with our hydration. This number allows the child to play the "How Low Can I Go?" game.

Let's go back to Bobby. After several months of working on his bowel health, Bobby has achieved much more bladder-friendly bowel health. It's not perfect, but he is pooping every day, and about half of the time he poops in the morning. His poop is definitely softer, and the story suggests he is likely emptying better. Mom confirms that his daytime bladder holds more, because Bobby has been drinking more in the mornings at breakfast and sometimes more during the morning at school, and he does not need to pee more often at school and no longer arrives home with urgency. On a recent ski trip, the parents didn't need to stop for Bobby to pee, and that was a first. Bobby has adjusted his evening fluids to stay hydrated, but he no longer consistently drinks excessively on hockey nights and weekends.

Mom now takes him to pee two hours after he falls asleep, and he is always dry at that time. The amount he pees is usually four or five ounces. He has dry mornings about a quarter of the time, and on those mornings, the amount he pees varies from four to seven ounces. Clearly, the amount his bladder will hold during the night has also increased. Adding up the averages of these two volumes on dry nights suggests that if Bobby makes no more than ten ounces of pee overnight, he can be dry when Mom takes him to pee when she goes to bed and again in the morning.

On the nights that he wets, Bobby pees two to seven ounces when he wakes up in the morning. Let's presume that when he wets, he pees about five ounces. If for every wet night we add how much he peed when Mom took him, plus five ounces in the pull-up, plus the amount when he peed first thing in the morning, we will get a good estimate of the range of how much pee he makes overnight. I do this for the last week on the calendar, and for Bobby, the amount of urine produced overnight on wet nights varied from eleven to seventeen ounces.

Since the most we know Bobby's bladder can currently hold is seven ounces, clearly we are still a long way from dryness without Mom's intervention at 10:30 p.m. However, Bobby can have more dry nights if he plays the "How Low Can I Go?" game. To win this game, Bobby needs to change his hydration to keep the overnight total as low as possible. The more he drinks before lunch and the more responsible he is in the evening, the lower the numbers and the more often he will wake up dry.

If the parent is up for the math and Bobby is up for the game, this exercise can help him learn how to manage his hydration to reduce his pee production overnight.

When parents want to do the math, I put an extra column on the calendar. The first pee column is the amount peed at bedtime, and this is mostly to prove that the child peed right at bedtime. The second column is the time when the parent took the child to pee. The third column is how much the child peed at this time. The fourth column is whether the child is wet or dry; the fifth column is the amount peed when the child wakes in the morning; and the sixth column is the total of the third and fifth columns on dry mornings and the total of the third and fifth columns and the estimated amount in the pull-up on wet mornings. The sixth column is the "How Low Can I Go?" game column.

Bobby	Date	Bedtime Pee Volume	Parent Take Time	Parent Take Volume	Wet W Dry D	First A.M. Volume	Total Volume
Mon	Nov 8						
Tue	9						
Wed	10						
Thu	11						
Fri	12						
Sat	13						
Sun	14						

Playing the "How Low Can I Go?" game is not for everyone, but I do ask all the parents to record the routine volumes and whether the child is wet or dry in the morning. I do the math myself at the follow-up appointments, and the numbers help me point out concerns with their hydration and whether they are making progress.

Playing the "How Low Can I Go?" game is not appropriate for the children who are going to bed dehydrated and who are not producing much urine overnight. Remember, the goal is dryness without thirst at bedtime and dryness without overnight dehydration. Ideally, I would like every child to be optimally hydrated all day, including in the evening and overnight. An optimally hydrated child should make an average of an ounce an hour while he sleeps. If a child is not making about an ounce an hour, I ask the parents to ensure that he is not going to bed thirsty and to increase his evening hydration as necessary to insure his kidneys can do their job overnight.

I thought of naming this chapter, "Bedwetting by Numbers."

What If I Do Nothing?

There are lots of good epidemiological studies that report on how common bedwetting is. There are good studies from North America, Europe, Japan, Hong Kong, Australia, and New Zealand. Bedwetting is present in all of these places in about 10 per cent of six-year olds, about 4 per cent of ten-year-olds, about 2 per cent of thirteen-year-olds, and about 1 per cent of adults. This refers to wetting at least once a week.[9]

These statistics suggest that a child who wets at six years of age has a 90 per cent chance of dryness as an adult. That sounds great so long as you are not one of the 10 per cent who will still be wetting as an adult.

If you are ten years old, the statistics suggest you have a 75 per cent chance of dryness as an adult, and if you are thirteen years old, you have a 50 per cent chance of dryness as an adult.

Doctors who tell parents that the child will likely become dry in time are therefore correct, but this is not much comfort for the families of a child who is always wet.

Wetting as an adult is a real problem. Studies have shown that wetting only once a month can have a negative effect on self-esteem in a child. Wetting once a month likely prevents an adult from looking for a live-together partner.

Parents would like to know when their child will be dry at night, and the statistics above don't help answer this question.

The only research statistic that does help is a study that showed that children who wet the bed every night in elementary school would likely still be wetting in adolescence. This statistic fits with my experience. If a child who

---

9   D. A. Bloom, W. W. Seeley, M. L. Ritchey, et al., "Toilet Habits and Continence in Children: An Opportunity Sampling in Search of Normal Parameters," *Journal of Urology* 149 (1993): 1087–90.

comes to my clinic is wetting every night, regardless of the age, we should not expect dryness in the short term. The parents should presume that without intervention, the wetting will still be present until at least adolescence.

Bedwetting does improve over time for at least four reasons. Each year, no matter how little the bladder holds, the body grows and so does the bladder. The bladder will hold a bit more—perhaps half an ounce to an ounce a year—and every ounce counts. Each year, the child will sleep a little less each night, and there will be less time for the bladder to fill up. During puberty, the pelvic volume will increase considerably, and this will minimize the poop wall effect. Finally, the ability to arouse (wake up) improves over time.

This is great if you are prepared to wait until adolescence, but if your child is wetting every night, waiting does not help, and you should do something.

So, the answer to the question at the head of this chapter is: if you do nothing and your child wets every night, nothing will likely change for a long time.

My recommendations work for children from the first grade to the last grade. Intervention always makes sense, and the younger you start, the earlier you will be dry. Younger children sometimes take longer to achieve dryness, but even if they took a year to achieve dryness, this makes much better sense than waiting.

Children who already have dry nights are more likely to be drier sooner without intervention, but there is a big difference between a child who is dry one night a week and a child who is dry half the nights. Half the nights really is close to dryness, but one night a week really isn't.

From my perspective, a child should be assessed and should be treated, even if he is only wetting once a week. In these children, I can achieve dryness promptly with only some fine-tuning of their hydration and pooping behaviours.

The most important reason to see a child who wets, regardless of how often the wetting occurs and how long the wetting is likely to persist, is to teach the child and family about the principles of good bladder health, bladder-friendly bowel health, and good hydration. These are important quality-of-life principles and offer benefits that are often as great and sometimes even greater than the joy of night dryness.

Why Not Use Medications?

There are three important reasons not to use medications.

1. Medications do not cure bedwetting.
2. Medications do not even control bedwetting very well.
3. Medications can cause side effects.

Only behavioural health therapy or time can *cure* bedwetting.

DDAVP

DDAVP (desmopressin) is the most commonly prescribed medication for bedwetting, and dryness every night is possible in only about 25 per cent of children. If the medication works, the child needs to stay on the medication until the wetting would otherwise resolve, which is often years. Until then, if the child stops taking the DDAVP, the wetting will return.

DDAVP has the best side-effect profile of all the medications. When this medication works, it does so by telling the kidneys to make less pee overnight. The most common reason why the medication does not work is because the bladder does not hold enough urine, and the medication cannot tell the kidneys to make a small enough amount of pee to fit in the bladder.

When DDAVP does work, it suggests that the bladder capacity is pretty good, and in my experience, many of these children can be dry with good hydration management. When a child comes to my office for the first visit and he is dry on DDAVP, this is a good prognostic feature for an early cure with behavioural health therapy, because this means that the amount that his bladder can hold is not super low.

If DDAVP works, with the correct dose, the medication will work from the first night and certainly within the first week. If there are no dry nights in the first week and if the child is on the maximal dose, there is no good reason to continue. Based on what the parents tell me, I suspect that some doctors and pharmacists believe that staying on the medication for longer periods will eventually result in dryness. This is not true.

Some mothers continue the DDAVP notwithstanding continued wetting because the medication results in less laundry. The child still wets the pull-up, but the sheets are dry. In my view, this is not a justifiable reason to stay on a medication. The soaking-through-the-pull-up problem can almost always be solved with modest changes in hydration management.

Some children initially have a positive response to DDAVP, and they have some dry nights, but over several weeks, the dry nights disappear. One reason to explain this pattern is that the body develops a "resistance" to the medication. There is some experimental evidence to suggest this might be the case. I have always thought that this "resistance" might be proof of the remarkable "intelligence" of our kidneys. My theory is that the DDAVP works initially, but that the body realizes that too much water is building up and that the kidneys, "brilliant" organs that they are, stop responding to the medication. In this situation, the kidneys are providing a protective response for the body. Unfortunately, sometimes the kidneys do not stop responding, and this can lead to a major side effect.

The only serious side effect with DDAVP is water intoxication, and this happens if you drink too much on the evenings when you take the medication or overnight. Most children with bedwetting try not to drink too much in the evening, so this is not a common side effect. However, some children do drink too much, and in these children, the fluid starts to build up in the body because the DDAVP tells the kidney not to make as much pee. Water intoxication develops when the water builds up too high, and this can happen even within a week of starting the medication. The early symptoms of water intoxication are headache and nausea, which is followed by vomiting, and this can be followed by seizure and coma. Ouch! Parents need to know that their child must be responsible about fluids on any evening he takes DDAVP.

Even though I don't prescribe DDAVP very often, I have a lot of experience with this medication. Before I learned how to cure children with behavioural health therapy, DDAVP was pretty much all I had to offer, and I learned a lot about it. I was always mindful of the side effect potential. In 1996, I published the first meta-analysis of the reports of water intoxication in children with enuresis who were treated with DDAVP. I published this with Dr. Jens Peter Norgaard, a prominent European paediatric urologist, in the *European Pediatric Journal*. A decade later, in 2006, Jens Peter and I published a follow-up meta-analysis in the *Journal of Urology*. These articles have helped focus the international medical community on the safe use of this medication. The 2006 article was especially important because this review helped establish that water intoxication was more common with the nasal spray form of DDAVP. Since our publication, the nasal spray formulation has been removed from the market in the United States. The nasal spray form of DDAVP should not be used to treat bedwetting.

DDAVP should be considered as a control therapy for special occasions, such as sleepovers, school trips, and sports camps. The medication generally results in consistent dryness only in those children who already have some dry nights. These children usually have a bladder that holds appreciably more than the children who wet every night. In these children, DDAVP might guarantee dryness and might make an important special occasion possible. I always ask parents to have the child take the medication for a week at some time before the special occasion to confirm whether the child will be consistently dry or not. I always use the maximal dose, which for the tablets is 0.6 milligrams (3 x 0.2 milligram tablets) and for the melts is 360 micrograms (3 x 120 microgram melts).

A child should never take more than the maximum recommended dose. I think some parents, and some doctors too, think that if a little helps, a lot will help more. This is wrong. The risk of water intoxication goes up when you take larger-than-recommended doses, because the duration of effect will extend into the next school day.

The medication should be taken at bedtime. The child must understand that he must not drink in the two hours before bedtime or overnight on the evenings when he takes DDAVP.

Touch wood, I have never had a child in my practice who developed water intoxication. But I am very careful to explain this risk to the child and the family. If I am not confident that a child will be responsible about evening fluid intake, I will not prescribe the medication. Most doctors who prescribe this medication do not tell parents about the risks. They should.

Imipramine

Imipramine (Tofranil) works more often than DDAVP, but still only results in dryness in about 35 per cent of children. If the medication works, the child needs to stay on the medication until the wetting would otherwise resolve, likely years. Until then, if the child stops taking the imipramine, the wetting will return.

Imipramine was one of the first generation of the antidepressant class of medications. I presume, but don't really know for sure, that the effect on bedwetting was discovered when patients who were depressed and who also wet the bed were treated with the medication for the depression and the bedwetting resolved.

How imipramine works is not clear. Side effects are common with imipramine. The most troublesome for parents is mood changes.

The biggest concern with this medication is that an overdose can be fatal. If the child who was treated with imipramine swallowed the whole bottle or if a younger sibling did or if a depressed adolescent sibling did or if a confused elderly grandparent did, these events might be fatal. For this reason, the World Health Organization (WHO) does not recommend imipramine for the treatment of bedwetting, and the ICCS recommends imipramine only as a third-line treatment and only with adequate precautions to prevent overdose.

I have a real personal aversion to this medication. When I was a young paediatrician, my department head asked me to be the acting director of the paediatric intensive care unit, and I served in this capacity for eighteen months. During that time, I personally turned off the ventilator of a child who suffered brain death due to poisoning with imipramine.

Oxybutynin and Tolterodine.

Oxybutynin (Ditropan) and tolterodine (Detrol) are used fairly commonly, but there are no well-controlled studies that show that these medications work at all!

The medication helps reduce bladder contractions and might presumably act to encourage the bladder to hold more.

Oxybutynin can cause constipation as well as other side effects. By now, I presume you have a good sense about how I would feel about using a medication that can cause bowel health to get worse.

There are other medications that act in a similar fashion and which are only approved for use in adults with overactive bladder syndrome.

Is It Possible to Cure Bedwetting in Children with ADHD, Learning Problems, or Autism?

Children with these problems can achieve dryness with my recommendations the same way children without these problems can achieve dryness.

Dryness can be achieved when a child works on the recommendations and when a parent provides the structure and support to encourage the child to sustain the effort. Older children might be well motivated, and this is a big asset, but so long as the child is compliant and works on the recommendations, success is possible.

I do not believe these problems per se are the big challenge in achieving dryness. Home and school routines are the challenge. Finding time to sit to poop in the morning is a big challenge. There are lots of parents of children with ADHD who make the time and provide the structure and who achieve the sacred morning poop. There are also lots of parents of children without a whiff of these problems, and they cannot make time for a morning poop. They do not improve. The same holds for every one of the many recommendations that I make.

Listening to children with Asperger's syndrome, children with "high end" autism, has helped me to learn about the relationship between bladder function and personality and behaviour. These children are intelligent, and bright children often have remarkable insights about their bodies—from the mouths of babes, as it were. Most of what I have learned over the years has come from listening to children and parents. I should dedicate this book to all those children and parents who have taught me how the bladder really works.

Children with autism have their own sense of the world. Unless you recommend something that makes sense to them, they will not consider the suggestion. Many of these children do not care what their peers or teachers think. They are quite happy to wet at school and continue to play in wet clothes.

One mother of a child with autism was very frustrated because her son would not work on the basics of good bladder and bowel health, and he continued to soak himself every day in grade two. The mom expressed her frustration pretty openly in the office, to my mind perhaps a bit too openly in front of the child, and this had become a regular theme with the follow-up visits. After several follow-ups without progress, the mom arrived with a smile and without complaint. I presumed her son had started to comply with some of the recommendations, but this was not the case. Mom described what happened.

"A few weeks ago, he came home from school soaked, and he never even bothered to try and change before he started to play. I lost it and started to cry. He was upset to see me crying, and he ran upstairs to his room. I presumed he was going to change his wet clothes. Instead, he came downstairs with one of his night diapers.

"'Mom,' he said, 'why don't I wear these to school?'"

The mom looked at me and commented, "He solved my problem."

The only thing that made sense to this boy was to solve his mother's problem, the problem of the wet clothes. The wetting at school was not his problem. He didn't personally care if he played in wet clothes, and he didn't personally care if he played in a wet pull-up either. He did care whether his mom was upset, and he found a solution when he saw his mom crying. Mom accepted this as a good interim solution. Sooner or later, these children decide to stay dry at school, but only when dryness makes personal sense to them, and of course, only once they have improved their bowel health.

Does Genetics Play a Role?

Bedwetting is common, and bedwetting in relatives is therefore also common. Many studies have reported that bedwetting can run in a family. Most parents who wet the bed as a child and who have a child who wets the bed relate that they presume their child has inherited the bedwetting.

I don't spend much time talking about genetics with parents. I've learned that talking about genetics is not usually helpful, can sometimes be unhelpful, and generally distracts the parent from what is important.

Researchers have identified three possible bedwetting genes. These genes are reported on chromosomes 13q, 12q, and 22q11. What might these genes control? They do not control bedwetting per se, but they might control some aspect of arousal, hydration, bowel health, or bladder health.

I can cure bedwetting in children with a family history of bedwetting and in children without a family history of bedwetting. A family history does not have any influence on whether a child will improve or not with my behavioural health recommendations.

The questionnaire that I ask families to fill out before the first visit has a question about whether any other family members wet the bed, but I do not discuss this unless a parent asks.

Many parents who wet the bed harbour feelings of guilt; they believe that they have caused the problem in their child. These parents often have bad memories about bedwetting as a child, and they are horrified to think these emotional scars might happen to their child. If I sense that a parent feels a sense of guilt, I tell the parent that I do not believe that genetics has anything to do with it. I tell these parents that bedwetting is so common that of course the problem can occur in several family members. I do my best to absolve these parents of any sense of guilt. As a general rule, parents who wet the bed and who had bad childhood memories about bedwetting seek help for their child at an earlier age than the average.

Most parents who wet the bed as a child and who bring their child to my office present as more considerate and patient with the problem than the average. This makes sense. These parents suffered the problem and would like to minimize the emotional impact in their child.

Occasionally, however, I come across a parent who wet the bed and who is not considerate or patient with the child. In this situation, the parent who did not wet the bed is almost always the parent who brings the child to the office. These parents often spontaneously share that their spouse has a "difficult time dealing" with the bedwetting. When I hear this, I make sure to spend some private time with the parent during the visit, and usually, I learn that the spouse gets mad and either emotionally or physically punishes the child for the bedwetting.

There is no role for punishment in the treatment of bedwetting, and I encourage the parent to protect the child from any form of abuse in the home, either from the spouse or from siblings. Bedwetting is bad enough without the added emotional burden of family criticism.

Many parents do not acknowledge that they wet the bed. They do not share this knowledge either with their spouse or with the child. I know this because over the years, many grandmothers have privately shared that the father or mother wet the bed, but that this parent refuses to acknowledge the history of wetting. Paternal grandmothers often share this with the daughter-in-law. I'm not always certain about the motivation of individuals who share this information within a family. Bedwetting in childhood often continues to have an emotional impact as an adult, and I always recommend that this issue be treated with the utmost discretion.

Having said that, if the emotional impact on the child is considerable and if one of the parents or grandparents did wet the bed and has not shared this with the child, and given that the spouse will be supportive and sympathetic, I encourage parents to share this information with their child. Children with bedwetting often feel alone with their problem. They often have no idea how many other children wet the bed. Learning that a parent also wet the bed and then became dry can be a major comfort and reassurance. Along the same lines, I routinely point out to children that the average-sized grade one or two class has two children who wet the bed. It helps to know you are not alone. Sometimes a grade-one child will respond, "Who is the other boy?"

How to Make Good Decisions about Pull-ups

Almost all children who wet the bed wish they did not have to wear a pull-up.

Many are embarrassed about the pull-ups. When friends come over, the evidence is hidden away in a closet. I recommend that parents store the pull-ups in a location where visitors will never see them. The closet in the child's bedroom is not discreet enough if friends come over to play.

Modern parents have a love-hate relationship with the pull-up. They hate the idea that their child is wearing the pull-up and some resent the cost, but these same parents welcome the lack of odour and laundry.

In a similar fashion, most children have mixed feelings about the pull-up. They are embarrassed to wear the pull-up, but they would rather not wake up in a stinky, wet bed.

Pull-ups are expensive, but so are sheets, mattresses, and laundry detergent. The time a mother spends on laundry is a major cost because this time prevents the mother from other activities that have a much higher value.

Pull-ups contain absorbent gels that are not organic; pull-ups are only slowly degradable and account for a sizable component of landfills.

Some children consider wearing a pull-up as a kind of punishment for something they cannot control. They would rather wake up in a wet bed and not wear a pull-up. However, their mother would like to avoid the odour and laundry. Some of these children plead with their mother to let them wet into the sheets.

I recollect a ten-year-old boy who made his feelings really clear in my office. During the first visit, the mother presented as very defensive about the pull-ups, and this almost always means the conversation has entered an emotionally sensitive area. I was watching the boy, and I could sense that he had something to say.

"How do you feel about wearing the pull-ups?" I asked as I looked at his sad face.

The boy broke eye contact, hung his head down, and replied, "I feel like a baby when I wear a pull-up."

Bedwetting can have negative effects on self-esteem. For this boy, wearing the pull-up likely had an additional and perhaps even more significant negative impact on his self-esteem than the bedwetting per se. That day, I cut a deal with the mother and the boy. He could stop wearing pull-ups if every morning, he would strip the bed, put the wet sheets into the washer, and help his mom put new sheets on the bed.

Sometimes parents differ about whether a child should wear a pull-up. The most common scenario is that the boy doesn't want to wear the pull-up, and the mom does want him to wear the pull-up. The father supports the son's position. The mother resents this because the father never does any of the laundry. I always feel as if I should somehow try to arbitrate this situation, but experience has taught me that the most I can usually do is commiserate with the mother.

Most children sleep through the night in a pull-up and never wake up. They don't wake up to pee during the partial arousal before the bladder empties. They don't wake up while the pee is coming out. They don't wake up later. The first time they know they have wet is when they wake up the next morning and take the pull-up off. This is the story whether the pull-up is a little wet or soaked, but this is not the story if the child soaks through the pull-up into the sheets.

Children who soak through into the sheets commonly wake up feeling wet and cold sometime later after the wetting. Some roll over and find a dry spot and fall back to sleep. Some take off the wet pull-up and put down new sheets or a towel and then go back to sleep. Some go to their mother, who performs these duties. Some take off the wet pull-up and crawl into bed with a parent or sibling. Some sleep on the floor, on the couch, or in the spare bedroom.

Waking up later is at least a sign that the child can wake up in the middle of the night. These children present as better on the arousal scale than children who never ever wake up, even when the parents describe the bed as a "swimming pool."

At some point, most parents try to stop the pull-ups with the hope that the wetting will go away. This almost never works when the bedwetting is a well-established nightly problem, but I don't discourage parents from trying.

If this strategy does work, it can only work by improving arousal. Stopping a pull-up is not likely to make the bladder hold more or to make the kidneys produce less pee.

What I suggest to parents is that if they would like to try to stop the pull-ups, they do this periodically for a period of up to two weeks at a time. After stopping the pull-ups, the parents should look for changes in arousal. If the child starts to wake up to pee during the partial arousal before the bladder empties, that is fantastic; the parents should of course stay the course. If the child starts to routinely wake up feeling wet and cold, and if by the end of the two weeks, there are occasional nights when the child wakes to pee in the middle of the night or wakes dry in the morning, then the parents should continue for longer than two weeks. However, if the child never wakes up at all, never wakes up to pee in the middle of the night, and never has a dry night, or if the only change is for the child to wake wet and cold, then I suggest that the child resume wearing pull-ups after the two-week trial. Parents could try this for two weeks every three to six months.

A pull-up should always be taken off as soon as the child wakes up in the morning. The mother might need to be present to wake up the child every morning to ensure this happens. Allowing a child to wear a pull-up while he plays in the morning is not a good practice. These children often pee in the pull-up while they play or watch television, and this is sending exactly the wrong message to the brain. I ask the child to never pee in the pull-up while he is awake. I explain that if he pees in the pull-up while he is awake, that this is like "practicing" wetting the bed. Similarly, a child should always put the pull up on as the last thing before bed, after voiding in the toilet.

Strategies for Camps
and for Sleepovers

A mom told me that the risk of bedwetting on a sleepover is a "damper" for the activity. She didn't realize she had used a pun in her comment.

Opportunities to attend a camp or school trip or sleepover come up while children are working on my recommendations but before they have achieved dryness. Sometimes the child is close enough to dryness that he can attend and be dry. This is generally only possible if the child has a bladder that holds a sufficient amount and if the child has already started to have some dry nights.

If a child has already achieved some dry nights, then the basic strategy is to make sure he attends to the basics of the morning poop and morning hydration, to ensure he is well hydrated at supper, to be very disciplined about not eating or drinking after supper, to stay up later, and always to pee immediately before lights out. These are the exception nights when a child is allowed to go to bed thirsty.

I commonly recommend DDAVP for these special occasions, but I always confirm this works before the child attends camp.

If the child is determined to attend camp and there is no hope of dryness, even with DDAVP, then the only alternative is to recruit one of the camp counsellors and to be incredibly discreet about the pull-ups. This is easier than most presume but requires planning. The counsellor should be instructed to put a pull-up in the bottom of the sleeping bag after all the children have left the sleeping area. When the child goes to bed, the child needs to silently put on the pull-up. Some pull-ups are less silent than others. The next morning, the child needs to return to the sleeping area when all the other children are away, put the pull-up in a plastic bag, put the bag in his daypack, go to the washroom, bury the pull-up in the garbage, and wash his hands carefully.

Some counsellors are prepared to handle the dispose-of-the-wet-pull-up duties. The sleeping bag should have an absorbent cotton liner, and the child should always wear pyjamas over the pull-up to help sop up any leakage and to protect the sleeping bag.

Some parents attend camps as coaches, counsellors, or volunteers, and this can really make a difference.

Bedwetting Is *Not* Due to a Psychological Problem

This is a myth that Freud has been blamed for, but I suspect the roots go back further at least to Victorian era England, when some considered bedwetting a sign of insanity.

This is nonsense.

Psychological concerns, when present at all, are either unrelated to the bedwetting, or more likely, are the result of the bedwetting.

Numerous studies confirm that bedwetting can have an appreciable negative impact on self-esteem. This is the main reason why bedwetting should be prevented or treated at an early age.

In the very uncommon situation when psychological problems are the cause, the wetting usually develops after a long period of dryness; the psychological cause is usually readily apparent; and the onset of the wetting usually closely follows the onset of the psychological cause. When wetting does develop after a prolonged period of dryness, sexual abuse should always be considered. A sexually abused child, who wets his bed, might do so to make the bed less attractive to the predator.

This is a good time for me to address punishment and bedwetting. There is no role for punishment in children with bedwetting. Sadly, every year, there are stories of a parent somewhere in North America who loses control and seriously harms or even kills a child who wets the bed.

Many parents try various forms of "discipline," which is a euphemism for punishment, and most stop when they realize that this intervention did not help, or they stop when they are asked to stop by a spouse, relative, friend, or medical professional.

Punishment has a very negative influence on the relationship between the child and the parent. Whenever I hear that a parent punishes the child, I make my position crystal clear. There is no role for punishment in the treatment of bedwetting.

Whenever I find evidence of physical abuse in a child I assess for bedwetting, I report the family to social services.

How to Prevent Bedwetting

Bedwetting can be prevented.

I've often thought that if I could teach every mother about the importance of bladder-friendly bowel health and how to perpetuate great bowel health from the first week of life, then there would be no need for physicians like me. I could teach my way out of my job!

The following are my recommendations to prevent bedwetting.

- I recommend breastfeeding for at least the first six months of life.
- I recommend water or juice supplementation when the temperature is warm or the child is in the sun.
- I recommend that parents minimize water losses from the body with humidifiers in dry climates.
- I recommend that parents minimize water loss from the skin by ensuring that their children are well covered when they are outside on a sunny day.
- After the child is weaned from the breast, I recommend that parents not overdo dairy products. An infant should enjoy enough dairy intake to satisfy the needs for calcium and vitamin D and for the essential fatty acids necessary for brain growth and development. Dairy products are not the only source of the essential fatty acids and are not necessarily the best source. Other sources of essential fatty acids include nuts, beans, lentils, eggs, and meat. The first three are also great sources of fibre.
- I recommend that every meal and snack have a fruit or vegetable; a healthy and substantial amount of fibre should be in every meal and snack. I recommend at least eighteen grams of fibre a day in

children up to three years of age and at least twenty-five grams in older children up to ten years of age and thirty to thirty-five grams in older children.

- I recommend that the child drink sufficient water and juice to ensure excellent hydration.
- Before the child is ready for toilet training, the parent should ensure that the poops are at least once a day in the morning and at the soft end of paste or mushy.
- Once a child is ready for toilet training, from the outset, the parents should encourage excellent posture with pooping and peeing. Children need an over-the-toilet seat and a footstool. Posture should continue as a parent-supervised/monitored project until the child fits an adult toilet.
- Once a child leaves home to attend day care or preschool, the parent needs to ensure that the morning poop routine is maintained.
- Parents should keep track of the bowel health of their child and should never presume that the child will poop when away from home.
- From the time that a child can walk, I recommend that the parent should wake the child up every morning and establish a routine such that the diaper is removed right away. The diaper should be put on right at bedtime—last thing on, first thing off.
- From the time a child is able to walk and sleep in a regular bed, there should be a night light in the room, in the corridor leading to the bathroom, and in the bathroom.
- If an infant or toddler wakes up and either calls to the mother or comes to her, the child should be instructed to pee before he climbs into bed with the mother or returns to his bed.
- If the child starts to wake up to pee, the mother should congratulate the child on this achievement so that the behaviour is reinforced.
- As soon as a child starts to pee in a potty, I recommend that the parents establish a routine that as soon as the night diaper is removed, the child is encouraged to immediately sit to pee on the potty.
- Infants and toddlers who will pee in the potty should be encouraged to pee when they wake, at common transition times, and always immediately before bed. Children should pee an average of six or seven times a day and should pee about every one and a half to two hours. I recommend that all boys sit to

pee at home. If boys stand to pee, the zipper or the pants must be pulled far enough down that the penis is not bent while the pee comes out.

- The goals of hydration for all children should be to get up and catch up with the hydration by drinking water or juice at breakfast, to keep up during the day, and to avoid late-afternoon and bedtime thirst. Fluids should not be restricted at bedtime.
- Parents should consider stopping diapers at a variety of common ages and milestones. They should stop the diapers for at least a week each time. Common times to stop include when the child starts to pee in the potty by day, when the child sleeps dry through an afternoon nap, and when a child starts to wake up in the middle of the night to either pee or come to the mother.

The End

One of my favourite quotes is from *Alice in Wonderland*.
The White Rabbit asks the king where to begin, and the king replies,

"Begin at the beginning,
and go on till you come to the end:
then stop."

Well, this is end of the book, but, I hope, the beginning of the journey to dryness for lots of children. Thank you for reading this book.

Brief Author Biography

Dr. Lane Robson has forty years of experience as a physician helping children and their families. He is a native Calgarian, and he graduated in the first medical class at the University of Calgary in 1973.

After completing fellowships in paediatrics and nephrology at the University of Toronto, he returned to Calgary in 1979, where he started the Division of Paediatric Nephrology at the University of Calgary. From 1993 to 2005, Dr. Robson worked, studied, taught, and did research abroad. During this time, he served in a variety of administrative and academic capacities, including professor of paediatrics at Brown University and professor of paediatric urology at the University of Oklahoma.

Dr. Robson has published more than six hundred papers. He serves on the editorial board of *Consultant for Pediatricians*, and he is a reviewer for more than a dozen international journals.

Lane Robson has received a variety of distinctions, including Teacher of the Year at Foothills Hospital in 1991, the Maternal and Child Health Award presented by the governor of the state of South Carolina in 1998, and an honorary master's degree from Brown University in 2001. He is a fellow of the Royal College of Physicians and Surgeons of Canada and Glasgow and a fellow of the Royal Society for Public Health.

The treatment of bedwetting in children has been Dr. Robson's main clinical interest for more than two decades. He has treated several thousands of children for this problem and has published more than sixty papers on this subject.

I Don't Intend to
Make Money with This Book

The price of this book is purposefully low to make the purchase as easy as possible for families. Any profits will be used to help with my charitable efforts as a paediatrician in poor countries, such as Haiti and Nicaragua.

Glossary of Medical Words

anal sphincter—A muscle that keeps the anus closed so that poop does not come out at the wrong time.

anus (bum hole)—This is the hole where the poop comes out.

bladder—A muscular sac at the bottom of the pelvis that holds the urine until we pee.

bowel (gut, intestine)—This is where the food is digested and where poop is made and stored.

cystitis—Infection in the bladder.

enuresis—This is the scientific name for bedwetting.

external sphincter—A muscle that circles the urethra, where the tube comes out of the bladder. This muscle closes off the urethra so that the urine does not leak out. The muscle must be consciously relaxed to let the pee come out.

frequency—This is a urine symptom that means a person voids more often than normal.

incontinence—This is the scientific name for leaking urine during the day.

kidneys—The organs that filter (clean) the blood and make urine from the waste products. There are two kidneys, one on each side at the top of the abdomen under the ribs.

neurogenic bladder—When the nerves from the spinal cord to the bladder are abnormal from birth or damaged because of an accident or disease, the bladder is no longer under normal nervous control, and this is referred to as a neurogenic bladder.

nocturia—This refers to waking up at night to pee.

pelvic floor muscles—These are the muscles that surround the anus and the urethra. These muscles need to relax for the bladder and the bowel to empty well.

pyelonephritis—Infection in the kidney.

rectum—The last part of the colon just before the poop comes out.

reflux—When the bladder contracts to empty, the hole where the ureter enters the bladder is meant to close so that urine in the bladder only goes out of the body and not back up to the kidney. If these holes do not close, the urine refluxes back up to the kidney. This is the most common physical abnormality that predisposes a child to kidney infection.

soiling—In this book, soiling refers only to poop accidents.

spinal cord—This is the bundle of nerves that runs down the spine. The lower spinal nerves control the muscles in the bladder and the bowel.

squatting—This is a learned strategy to prevent a soaking episode. The girl suddenly drops down into a crouch with her heel pressed into the genital area. There will always be some dampness. Squatting is a dangerous symptom because the pressure in the bladder during a squat is very high and over time this can damage the bladder.

stool (poop)—What is left after food has been digested.

ureter—The tubes that carry the urine from the kidneys to the bladder.

urethra—The tube that carries the urine from the bladder outside of the body.

urgency—This refers to the race to the bathroom that is so common in children. These children feel an "urgent" need to get to the bathroom before the urine comes out. This implies the bladder is up against the poop wall.

urinary tract infection—This refers to infection in the kidneys or in the bladder.

urine (pee)—The kidney filters (cleans) the blood and regulates our salt and water balance by making urine.

withholding—When a child says no to the signal to poop, this is referred to as withholding.

History of Bedwetting

Some of the first medical texts ever written included treatments for bedwetting. The Ebers Papyrus of Egypt, which dates from 1550 BC, suggested a combination of a vegetable and a mineral salt in a fluid vehicle, such as water, beer, or honey as a treatment for bedwetting.

The bedwetting alarm was discovered more than a century ago, in 1904, by a German physician named Pfaundler, who was in charge of a home for handicapped children. Some of the children wet at night, and they developed rashes from sleeping in their urine. Dr. Pfaundler designed a simple alarm that would go off when the bed was wet so that a nurse could promptly change the child. They discovered, however, that some of the children stopped wetting! In the thirties, O. H. Mowrer and Willie Mae Mowrer, two Yale psychologists, a husband and wife team, studied alarm therapy in bedwetting and confirmed the effectiveness.

Overproduction of urine during the night has been reported as a cause of bedwetting since the nineteenth century. During the first half of the twentieth century, physicians understood that there was a hormone in the pituitary that controlled the production of urine. This hormone was called antidiuretic hormone. "Anti" means "against," and "diuretic" means "to make pee." This hormone reduced the production of urine. Doctors wondered if this hormone would be useful in the treatment of bedwetting, and a *Lancet* article from 1956 reported the use of pituitary snuff, a desiccated product obtained from cattle pituitary, for bedwetting. They clearly didn't know about mad cow disease back then! Once the exact chemical was isolated, Ferring Pharmaceuticals produced a synthetic form, desmopressin (DDAVP), and this has been used to treat bedwetting since the 1960s. This was the biggest advance since the discovery of the bedwetting alarm, and this ushered in the overproduction-of-urine-research era.

During the 1990s, several physicians around the world started to report that the bladder capacity was reduced in children with bedwetting. Gil Rushton, one of the top paediatric urologists in the world and the current editor of the paediatric articles in the *Journal of Urology*, was one of the first to report this important factor.[10] Gil Rushton and I served on the National Kidney Foundation Bedwetting Committee for about a decade. C. K. Yeung also published research that showed the importance of bladder capacity. This ushered in the bladder-capacity-research era.

The International Children's Continence Society (ICCS) was formed in 1997, with Kelm Hjälmås as the first president. This important group has supported research and education on bedwetting, and during the last two decades, our understanding of bedwetting has improved substantially.

10 H. G. Rushton, A. B. Belman, M. R. Zaontz, S. J. Skoog, and S. Sihelnik, "The Influence of Small Functional Bladder Capacity and Other Predictors on the Response to Desmopressin in the Management of Monosymptomatic Nocturnal Enuresis," *Journal of Urology* 156 (1996): 651–6.

References

These are the citations for some of my most important articles and also important articles written by other physicians, most of whom I know and all of whom I respect.

Robson, W. L. M. 2009. "Evaluation and Management of Enuresis." *New England Journal of Medicine* 360:1429–36.

Robson, W. L. M. 2008. "Current Management of Nocturnal Enuresis." *Current Opinion in Urology* 18:425–30.

Robson, W. L. M., A. K. C. Leung, and J. P. Norgaard. 2007. "The Comparative Safety of Oral Versus Intranasal Desmopressin in the Treatment of Children with Nocturnal Enuresis." *Journal of Urology* 178:24–30.

Robson, W. L. M., A. K. C. Leung, and R. van Howe. 2005. "Primary and Secondary Nocturnal Enuresis: Similarities in Presentation." *Pediatrics* 115:956–9.

Robson, W. L. M., and A. K. C. Leung. 2004. "A Survey of Voiding Dysfunction in Children with Attention Deficit Hyperactivity Disorder." *Journal of Urology* 172:388–9.

Robson, W. L. M., and A. K. Leung. 2002. "Urotherapy Recommendations for Bedwetting." *Journal of the National Medical Association* 94:577–80.

Robson, W. L. M., and A. K. C. Leung. 2000. "Secondary Nocturnal Enuresis." *Clinical Pediatrics* 39:379–85.

Robson, W. L. M., H. P. Jackson, D. Blackhurst, A. K. C. Leung. 1997. "Enuresis in Children with Attention-Deficit Hyperactivity Disorder." *Southern Medical Journal* 90:503–5.

Robson, W. L. M., J. P. Norgaard, and A. K. C. Leung. 1996. "Hyponatremia in Patients with Nocturnal Enuresis Treated with DDAVP." *European Journal of Pediatrics* 155:959–61.

Bael, A. M., H. Lax, H. Kirche, et al. 2006. "Reference Ranges for Cystographic Bladder Capacity in Children—with Special Attention to Vesico-Ureteral Reflux." *Journal of Urology* 176:1596–1600. (The bladder capacity graph was derived from Dr. Bael's data. Thank you, Dr. Bael.)

Bakker, E., J. D. van Gool, M. van Sprundel, et al. 2002. "Results of a Questionnaire Evaluating the Effects of Different Methods of Toilet Training on Achieving Bladder Control." *British Journal of Urology* 90:456–61. (All three articles by Bakker provide historical evidence for the importance of my good bladder health recommendations. Dr. van Gool has contributed a huge amount to our understanding of bladder function in childhood.)

Bakker, E., J. van Gool, and J. J. Wyndaele. 2001. "Results of a Questionnaire Evaluating Different Aspects of Personal and Familial Situation, and the Methods of Potty-Training in Two Groups of Children with a Different Outcome of Bladder Control." *Scandinavian Journal of Urology and Nephrology* 35:370–6.

Bakker, E., and J. Wyndaele. 2000. "Changes in the Toilet Training of Children during the Last 60 Years: The Cause of an Increase in Lower Urinary Tract Dysfunction?" *British Journal of Urology* 86:248–52.

Bloom, D. A., W. W. Seeley, M. L. Ritchey, et al. 1993. "Toilet Habits and Continence in Children: An Opportunity Sampling in Search of Normal Parameters." *Journal of Urology* 149:1087–90. (Dr. David Bloom is one of the foremost paediatric urology docs of my generation.)

Butler, R. J., and J. Heron. 2007. "The Prevalence of Infrequent Bedwetting and Nocturnal Enuresis in Childhood. A Large British Cohort." *Scandinavian Journal of Urology and Nephrology* 42:1–8. (Dr. Richard Butler is a British psychologist and a world authority on bedwetting alarm therapy.)

Butler, R. J., P. Holland, S. Gasson, et al. 2007. "Exploring Potential Mechanisms in Alarm Treatment for Primary Nocturnal Enuresis." *Scandinavian Journal of Urology and Nephrology* 41:407–13.

Byrd, R. S., M. Weitzman, N. E. Lanphear, et al. 1996. "Bed-wetting in US children: Epidemiology and Related Behavior Problems." *Pediatrics* 98:414–9.

Glazener, C. M. 2005. "Alarm Interventions for Nocturnal Enuresis in Children." *Cochrane Database of Systematic Reviews* Art. No.: CD002911. DOI: 10.1002/14651858, CD002911.pub2.

Glazener, C. M., and J. H. Evans. 2002. "Desmopressin for Nocturnal Enuresis." *Cochrane Database Systematic Revue* (3):CD002112. (The three articles by Glazener summarize the very best meta-analysis references for the effectiveness of the various therapies.)

Glazener, C. M., and J. H. Evans. 2000. "Tricyclic and Related Drugs for Nocturnal Enuresis in Children." *Cochrane Database Systematic Revue* (2):CD002117.

Hägglöf, B., O. Andrán, E. Bergstöm, et al. 1997. "Self-Esteem before and after Treatment in Children with Nocturnal Enuresis and Urinary Incontinence." *Scandinavian Journal of Urology and Nephrology* 31:79–82.

Joensson, I. M., C. Siggaard, S. Rittig, et al. 2008. "Transabdominial Ultrasound of Rectum as a Diagnostic Tool in Childhood Constipation." *Journal of Urology* 179:1997–2002. (Dr. Soren Rittig, from Aarhus, Denmark, and his group at the International Enuresis Research Center have done some of the finest research in the world on bedwetting.)

Loening-Baucke, V., and D. S. Pashankar. 2006. "A Randomized, Prospective, Comparison Study of Polyethylene Glycol 3350 without Electrolytes and Milk of Magnesia for Children with Constipation and Fecal Incontinence." *Pediatrics* 118:528–35.

Longstaffe, S., M. E. K. Moffatt, and J. C. Whalen. 2000. "Behavioral and Self-Concept Changes after Six Months of Enuresis Treatment: A Randomized Controlled Trial." *Pediatrics* 105:935–40.

McGrath, K. H., P. H. Y. Caldwell, and M. P. Jones. 2008. "The Frequency of Constipation in Children with Nocturnal Enuresis: A Comparison of Parental Reporting." *Journal of Paediatric Child Health* 44:19–27.

Nevéus, T., P. Eggert, J. Evans, et al. 2008. "Evaluation and Treatment of Monosymptomatic Enuresis—A Standardization Document from the International Children's Continence Society (ICCS)." ICCS Website, www.i-c-c-s.org. (Dr. Tryg Neveus, from Stockholm, is the current secretary of the International Children's Continence Society and one of the foremost experts on bedwetting in the world.)

Nevéus, T., G. Läckgren, T. Tuvemo, et al. 2000. "Enuresis Background and Treatment." *Scandinavian Journal of Urology and Nephrology* 34:1–44.

Nevéus, T., A. von Gontard, P. Hoebeke, et al. 2006. "The Standardization of Terminology of Lower Urinary Tract Function in Children and Adolescents: Report from the Standardization Committee of the International Children's Continence Society." *Journal of Urology* 176:314–24. (Dr. Alexander von Gontard is a child psychiatrist and wonderful fellow. He is *the* psychiatrist in the bedwetting world.)

Norgaard, J. P., E. B. Pedersen, et al. 1985. "Diurnal Antidiuretic Levels in Enuretics." *Journal of Urology* 134:1039–42.

Nurko, S., N. N. Youssef, et al. 2008. "PEG3350 in the Treatment of Childhood Constipation: A Multicenter, Double-Blinded, Placebo-Controlled Trial." *Journal of Pediatrics* 153:254–61.

Rushton, H. G., A. B. Belman, M. R. Zaontz, S. J. Skoog, and S. Sihelnik. 1996. "The Influence of Small Functional Bladder Capacity and Other Predictors on the Response to Desmopressin in the Management of Monosymptomatic Nocturnal Enuresis." *Journal of Urology* 156:651–6.

Index

European Pediatric Journal, 135
evening surge, 42, 43, 121, 123, 124, 128
external sphincter, 90, 123, 155
extract of senna (Sennakot), 74

F

fat, 70
feet, position of while emptying, 63
fever, 85
Fibersure (inulin), 74, 75
fibre
    content of common foods, 67–70
    recommendations for, 66, 149–150
    sources of, 149
    and stool consistency, 66
    supplements, 75–79
first contact, described, 36
floor potty, 19
fluid intake, 42, 51, 73, 151. *See also*
    hydration
footpads-beside-the-hole solution, 18
footstools, to help children position feet
    while emptying, 63
foreskin and foreskin care, 52, 93, 94
frequency, as urine symptom, 34, 85, 155
Freud, Sigmund, 147
fruits, recommendations for, 66, 149
full bladder signals, 8

G

gastro-colic reflex, 15
genetics, and bedwetting, 140
genitals and genital hygiene, 52, 86, 89, 91,
    92, 93, 156
getting out of bed at night, reasons why
    child does not, 8
girls, guidelines for good bladder health, 29
glossary, 155–156
good bladder health
    guidelines for boys, 28
    guidelines for girls, 29
GoodNite™, 49

H

hard poop, 13, 42, 47, 70, 79, 112

health insurance plans, and alarm therapy,
    103
hemorrhagic cystitis, 85
Hjälmås, Kelm, 54, 158
holding
    belief about, 32
    consequences of, 33
hot tubs, cautions/concerns with, 93
"How Low Can I Go?" (game), 129, 130
humidifiers, 149
hydration. *See also* fluid intake
    and amount of pee kidneys make, 124,
        126
    assessing level of, 129–131
    case example of, 95–98
    effects of great hydration, 71, 74, 82
    effects of milk on, 70
    and genetics, 140
    goals of, 151
    managing at school, 43
    proper hydration, 54
    recommendations for, 72–73, 78, 150
    reward for, 118
    rules of, 96
    and soaking-through-the-pull-up
        problem, 135
    and stool consistency, 66, 75, 78

I

ice cream, 70
imipramine (Tofranil), 136–137
In the Realm of Hungry Ghosts (Mate), 36
incontinence, 155
International Children's Continence Society
    (ICCS), 48, 51, 137, 158
inulin (Fibersure), 74, 75

J

Journal of Urology, 135, 158

K

kidney infections, 85–86
kidneys
    and DDAVP, 134–135
    described, 39, 40, 155
    holding on to water, 51

urine test
  at doctor visit, 50–51
  at home, for testing for bladder
    infections, 87–88, 89
Uroflow curve, 49, 52
Uroflow toilet, 23, 24, 63
urotherapy, 54

V

vegetables, recommendations for, 66, 149
Victorian era, 18, 19, 86, 147
video games, 27, 36, 60
vitamin D, 149
voiding, discomfort with, as evidence of
  bladder infections, 85

W

Warzak, Bill, 54
water, amount of, in body, 39–40
water bottles, at school, 43, 73, 97
water closet (WC), 18
weekend poopers, 21
"Wii wee," 27
wiping issue, 53
withholding
  as cause of bowel problem, 16, 57
  described, 16–17, 156
  and leaving home, 20
Wolters, Judith Spungen, 66n
World Health Organization (WHO), 137

Y

Yeung, C. K., 6, 158

Made in the USA
Coppell, TX
07 December 2019

12511886R00105